THE STEPMOTHER IN FAIRY TALES
Bereavement and the Feminine Shadow

D1615978

THE STEPMOTHER IN FAIRY TALES
Bereavement and the Feminine Shadow

JACQUELINE M. SCHECTMAN

SIGO PRESS
BOSTON

SIGO PRESS
25 New Chardon Street, #8748
Boston, Massachusetts 02114

Publisher and General Editor Sisa Sternback

Library of Congress Cataloging-in-Publication Data

Schectman, Jacqueline M.,
        The stepmother in fairy tales : bereavement and the feminine shadow / Jacqueline M. Schectman.
            p.   cm.
        Includes bibliographical references.
        ISBN (invalid) 0-933434-78-0 (cloth) $29.95. — ISBN (invalid) 0-933434-77-2 (pbk.) : $16.95
        1. Fairy tales—History and criticism.   2. Stepmothers—Folkore.   3. Loss (Psychology).   4. Psychoanalysis and folklore.   5. Jung, C. G. (Carl Gustav), 1875-1961. I. Title.
        GR471.S34   1993
        398'.042—dc20   93—6713
                                                                            CIP

Printed in Korea.

For
Lena Kanofsky
Helen Krieger Richman
Rebecca Kanofsky Richman
and Dark Mothers Everywhere

ACKNOWLEDGEMENTS

Many thanks are due to those who have contributed to this work, from conception to delivery. Several years ago, Robert Bosnak held the mirror for Snow White's Evil Queen as she appeared in my middle-aged dreams, and welcomed her archetypal presence to our work. A few years later Winona Hubrecht introduced "The Laidly Worm of Spindlestone Heugh"—the first tale in this work—to analytic trainees in a wonderfully rich seminar. I was asked to amplify the image of The Stepmother, and my interest was kindled in other Stepmother tales; the Evil Queen, I saw, could take many forms, work all sorts of dark magic. My fascination with her grew.

Ethne Grey gave me the opportunity to present some half-formed ideas to The Boston Friends of Jung in the Spring of 1988; the enthusiasm of that group impelled me onward, and many of their thoughts on the material have been incorporated in the work, along with the heartfelt responses of other groups I've met with in the intervening years.

As I began to write, good friends were subjected to draft after draft, as I drew them into my obsession. Joe and Louise Cambray and Jane Pretat were patient and free with their support and their suggestions, almost all of which brought light to the murky darkness of my explorations.

PREFACE

The usual approach of Jungian writers to the important theme of the mother, or stepmother, in fairy tales has been to interpret her as a power within the psyche, an archetypal force or complex which it is the task of the hero or heroine to confront or to escape from. This prevailing view goes back to Jung's discovery of the archetype of the "terrible mother" with her life-or-death challenge to consciousness and psychological growth, a challenge that is enacted in myths throughout the world. Hence, we have become accustomed to thinking of such figures in fairy tales as fateful inner powers which must be met and dealt with in the life work of psychological development and individuation.

As modern writers on fairy tales have helped to make us aware, however, the roles which we assign to the various types of fairy tale characters have a profound effect on the way we perceive their real-life counterparts. If I see the "wicked stepmother" only as an obstacle to the hero's way, or even as a necessary challenge to the hero, I will unconsciously carry this perception over to women in my life. Thus, the actual female person becomes, in my perception, a "witch," a negative archetypal force. So, such a view of a fairy tale character can contribute subtly, but deeply, to a distortion of experience and to an impoverishment and rigidity in relationships. The resulting projection onto a woman is also untrue, unfair and in urgent need of correction.

Jacqueline Schectman's book is an extraordinary step out of this entrenched false position. She has gone inside the mind and heart of the "wicked stepmother" to discover, and beautifully elucidate, feelings, behavior and responses which belong not only to mothers and stepmothers, but to all of us. With an artful interweaving of fairy tale and clinical material, she draws many of the fine and subtle shadings that characterize what is in essence a state of mind, showing how and when it arises in our experience and the often paradoxical ways in which it hinders or furthers our growth.

The reader will encounter here a whole new view of the so-called negative feminine. For the humor, understanding and compassion which Jacqueline Schectman brings to this theme, we owe her an enormous debt.

David Hart, Ph.D.

INTRODUCTION

In 1990 and for several years before completion of this book, one could hardly read a newspaper or watch the evening news without learning of some horrifying incident of child abuse. As if a heavy lid had been lifted from a dreadful box of woes, the long held secrets of assaulted children and their parents filled the air. Religious groups and family service agencies dramatized the daily wounds of family life, while twelve-step groups for "adult children" of abuse continued to be formed in every city and town. When Miller (1981) and Masson (1984) urged depth psychologists to listen once again to the trauma of their patients' early lives, therapists of every sort learned to see the wounded child in the adult seeking help.[1]

Collective consciousness has found little difficulty in identifying with this wounded child. Who among us has not, after all, felt put upon, abandoned, and deprived at some time while growing up? The wounding parent, on the other hand, has been much more difficult to own. Violent, abandoning, sadistic parents have been seen as a new scourge upon the earth, as strangers from some distant, unknown realm. Viewed as a trou-

---

[1]Every paper presented at the October, 1990, National Conference of Jungian Analysts dealt, in some way, with the issue of the wounded child. The previous conference, in 1988, focused entirely on the family.

bling sociological phenomeon, these parents are perceived as products of a driven, narcissistic age, manifestations of a godless society, the inevitable result of splintered family life. They are criminal, or to be pitied, surely having been abused themselves. They are not like us.

In the face of such distancing denial, fairy tales present a most disturbing truth: mistreated children have been with us for as long as families have told their tales. Cinderella (and her sisters!) suffer terrible abuse; Hansel and Gretel are left starving in the woods; Snow White cannot escape her stepmother's jealous wrath. While acknowledging abuse, however, these tales also offer a collective escape hatch, a means of denying the *proximity* of the abuser. In fairy tales, one seldom sees real parents visiting mayhem on their children; the damage is done by shadowy counterparts. Cannibalistic giants and ogres stand in for bad fathers, and, more frequently, the Wicked Stepmother carries the role of the dark, envious, vengeful mother. Natural parents, the tales seem to say, would never treat their children in that way.

There is evidence that the Grimm brothers changed "Mother" to "Stepmother" in transcribing most of the child abuse tales; they apparently wished to protect and preserve the image of Good Motherhood to make the tales easier to read and hear (Tatar, 1987).[2] These changes, it would seem, were not arbitrary, but consistent with tales from around the world, in which Stepmothers have always appeared as sources of terror in a child's imaginary world.

Bettelheim (1977) sees the Mother/Stepmother dichotomy as a device that allows for a gradual integration of the dark forces of the unconscious. Until a child (of any age) has enough ego strength to carry his own ambivalence, he can love the good and nurturing mother while thinking of the scolding and withholding one as a hateful stranger. The tales allow the child to take the negative mother into consciousness as a developing tolerance for her permits.

---

[2]Two exceptions that come to mind are "The Raven" (#93) and "The Seven Ravens" (#25), in which natural, impatient and ultimately regretful parents wish their children into birds who fly away.

The image of the Stepmother as intruder in the happy home is in keeping with family experience of her. A mother caught in Stepmother's archetypal power feels possessed, invaded by an alien being. Her patience and tolerance are gone; she has nothing left to give; envy is all that she can feel. The Good-and-Loving-Mother dies a swift, if temporary, death while Stepmother wails out a lament:

> "I don't know what happened; it was some wild banshee screaming at those kids!"

> "I was beside myself. I wanted to kill them!"

> "I thought, `That's not my child'"

Children surely recognize Stepmother's presence in the home. A woman recalls rifling through her mother's desk when she was a child, searching for the adoption papers she was certain she would find. The hateful woman who claimed to be her mom could not *really* be her relative by blood!

Whether one views the Stepmother from the perspective of the parent or the child, it seems necessary to keep her at a distance, to hold her at psychological arm's length until one feels strong enough to take her on, or to take her in. The fairy tales in which she plays a major role offer an opportunity to do both. When reading these tales from her point of view, watching her dark and rageful movements with an empathetic eye, one need not be so fearful of her witch-like power. Unlike the Thirteenth Fairy in "Little Briar Rose,"[3] Stepmother will have been invited to the feast.

We might begin this move toward empathy with an understanding of her name. The Step- in Stepmother derives from the Middle English *steif,* meaning bereaved, and was originally applied to orphaned children. A Stepmother, then, is the mother of a bereaved child. Loss and grief are her milieu, her *raison d'etre.* In fairy tales she arrives in the face of death, summoned

---

[3] A story better known, perhaps, as "Sleeping Beauty" (Grimms #50).

by the family's loss. Often, through her dark machinations, evil is turned upon itself and grief is finally resolved. She is the force that moves the bereaved child beyond tears and into action on his own behalf. But she is more than an agent of heroic growth and change; she is a *creature* of the grief in which she moves, a shadow figure rising not *ex nihilo,* but out of wrenching loss. To know this is to begin to understand her in ourselves.

My personal interest in the archetypal Stepmother began around a double bereavement: I was losing my youth, and I was about to lose my younger child. In the summer of my fortieth year I moved into a small Boston apartment with my seventeen-year-old daughter. She would be leaving for college in the fall, but in the interim we were together, in very close quarters. While all was well on the surface—I'd planned for this moment for many years—my dreams were full of rage, full of envy of my daughter's beauty and vitality. In one such dream she'd taken all of my bright, silky clothes and put them on a high closet shelf, just out of my reach. I was left standing in faded polyester, screaming at my mirror. My analyst observed: "Now you know about Snow White's Mother," and so I did. I felt an immediate connection to the terrible Stepmother/Queen and considerable comfort in recognizing her archetypal presence in my dreams. The work with her allowed me to let go of my daughter (slowly) while maintaining some sort of dialogue with my truth-telling mirror.

On a professional level, I've come to know the Stepmother all too well in my countertransferential response to the children in my practice. To the degree that these children have experienced abuse, neglect and abandonment in their lives, they demand the presence of the Stepmother in the playroom. She is an irreducible part of their bereavement and they will work and work at my limits until they have brought her into the hour. The great challenge of the work then is in allowing her entry, and in keeping her in consciousness long enough to address her presence, often with the telling and retelling of her tales. She must not, of course, be allowed to act on her murderous desires. This challenge must be met with each new hour, but treated with due respect the Stepmother can serve as she does in fairy tales. She is a force against which the child can test his growing strength and maturity.[4]

My approach to fairy tales is a reflection of my work with families and young children in that I tend to read the tales as bridges between inner and outer life, as stories of the struggle to find and define one's place in the world. For the child, that world begins with family, and fairy tales are experienced as metaphors for family life; they present the developmental tasks of life in relationship. Thus, my reading of a tale is likely to focus first on its implications for relationship, for family dynamics: why has Good Mother died, what sort of loss has brought Stepmother to the scene? What might this family be like, seen through Stepmother's eyes? This treatment, while not excluding the reading of the fairy tale as subjective inner drama, adds the contextual dimension of outer life.

To reread Stepmother tales from the Stepmother's point of view is to turn the stories upside down, shaking loose new meaning from within. "Snow White", then, is not just a romance of a young girl's passage into life, but a story of a woman's bitter battle against time, against the aging and decline that come with middle age. It speaks to the envy and frustration that separate a woman from her youth. "Hansel and Gretel", more than a survivor's tale, serves as a primer on "bad" mothering, on the seductions and betrayals present in the raising of a child. At times of "famine in the land," when mother has nothing left to give, she may try to lose her children in the woods, hoping with all her heart that they will not return; or, perhaps to defend against this cold rejecting one, she may keep her children close to her within her milk-and-cookies house, only to devour them in time.

In "Cinderella", a tale in which the women share the loss of a father's love, the notion of Good Mothering is turned on end. While Stepmother offers Cinderella grueling tasks and hard

---

[4]The therapist who knows her own Stepmother well can relate to her patients' parents in a very different way; she begins to see their "badness," at least in part, as a product of the strains of daily life. Freed of her own perfect parent fantasies, she can see her patients (and help them to see themselves) in the context of relationships that they, in some small ways, can change.

advice, these dark gifts prepare Cinderella for her prince. Her pampered sisters, on the other hand, suffer greatly from their mother's love. In "The Laidly Worm...", the less familiar tale with which this book begins, the Witch/Stepmother/Queen is brought to the story by the kingdom's loss. She is the essence of bereavement, carrying grief in all its awful power to transform. She survives in the form of a loathsome toad, croaking the kingdom into consciousness. This evil Queen of Bamborough Keep is a Stepmother one can love to hate.

A clarifying note may be in order here. When I refer to the Good Mother, to the Stepmother, to bereavement, I refer to impersonal, archetypal forces, psychological states that belong to no one, and to everyone. The Good Mother/Stepmother in imagination may wear the clothing of personal experience, may affect us in profoundly personal ways, but she is not to be confused with the personal mother or stepmother. (This book is not about those brave souls who try to raise other people's children.) When The Stepmother makes her presence felt she is neither mine nor yours; she simply is, and we are all caught in her power.

Let us proceed to read her tales.

1

BEREAVEMENT AND THE STEPMOTHER
"THE LAIDLY WORM OF SPINDLESTON HEUGH"

Webster's New Twentieth Century Dictionary defines bereavement as a state of deprivation; as loss, particularly through death, of a friend or relative. To bereave is to strip, to divest, to dispossess; to be bereft is to be left sad and alone. The term implies destitution and affliction, mourning *and* melancholia. Bereavement is the lived experience of grief.

Stepmother tales are stories of bereavement, of loss and of the working through of loss. They speak to the dark aspects of the psyche constellated by deep grief: rage, envy and despair; the desire for revenge; the wish to alter harsh reality by whatever magic comes to hand. These fairy tales take us through the process of bereavement in mythopoetic form, with Stepmother at center stage, casting her dark spells and screaming out her rage.[1]

---

[1]Bowlby, in his definitive work on *Attachment and Loss* (New York, Basic Books, 1980: Vol.3,85) outlines the phases of bereavement:

1. Numbing that may be interrupted by outbursts of intense distress and/or anger.
2. Yearning and searching for the lost object; anger.
3. Disorganization and despair.
4. Reorganization and reorientation to reality.

In fairy tale language, we might restate the phases thus:

1. The kingdom suffers a terrible loss, and the Good Queen dies of grief.

(continued on page 2)

The following Stepmother tale, "The Laidly Worm of Spindleston Heugh,"[2] provides a screen for viewing the effects of grief on family life. In particular, it speaks to the grief of mothers who must let their children go. Even in fairy tales, family life is strained by leave-takings and losses that may "kill" the nurturing Mother, making way for the Dark One to enter in her stead. Bereavement does not require a literal death. Every passage through a stage of life, each initiation with its implications for rebirth, is a sort of death as well, an occasion to invite Stepmother to the scene.

The story begins in peace and tranquility, with a portrait of the royal family:

> *In Bamborough Castle once lived a king who had a fair wife and two children, a son named Childe Wynd and a daughter named Margaret.*

They could be any family, son and daughter, mom and dad, balanced and complete. One might wish to suspend this unity in time, to preserve the harmony implicit here, but families inevitably change with time. One day, as adventurous young princes must,

> *Childe Wynd went forth to seek his fortune...*

An illustration in a children's version of this tale shows a stiff-backed Queen, standing in profile, watching a small ship sail toward the horizon. One can imagine the sadness in the

---

(continued from page 1)

2. A new Queen is sought and found but she is evil, an enchantress.

3. The Witch/Stepmother/Queen,caught up in envy and in rage, wreaks havoc in the kingdom and upon her family.

4. Her Stepchildren rally around, perform heroic deeds and depotentiate the Witch. The kingdom is restored to new levels of harmony.

[2]The text used here (see appendix A) is taken from *English Fairy Tales,* collected by Joseph Jacobs (New York, Schocken). The illustrations I refer to accompany the retelling of the tale by D. Weisner and K. Kahng, *The Loathsome Dragon* (New York, Putnam: 1987).

moment, feel the loss, as the hero's journey is experienced from Mother's point of view. For Childe Wynd it is the beginning of his life as a man. For the Queen, it is the end of a part of her life:

> *...soon after he had gone, his mother, the Queen, died.*

In primitive tribes, women keen and wail as their sons leave the mothers' lodge to march off to their initiation rites. The young men have made their break with childhood, with the maternal world, and they are mourned as dead. "The mothers have the foreboding that the boys will never again be what they were before initiation: their children." (Eliade, 1958:8) One can see this scene replayed in small ways at every kindergarten school bus stop, at the doors of any preschool as a child lets go of mother's hand and runs off to join his friends. Whenever children turn their backs on mother love and move bravely into life, some part of mother dies, even as she smiles in admiring pride and waves goodbye.

I recall my son's *Bar Mitzva* with pleasure and with pain. I'd not truly understood the initiatory nature of the rite, but on the Friday evening preceding the big day, some of this understanding must have reached my son. Standing in a crush of relatives and friends he began to cry, and before I could reach him in the crowd his father, grandfather and cousins gathered round to comfort him with stories of their own *Bar Mitzva* days. My son soon began to laugh—I watched this from a distance—and I experienced a terrible sense of my own obsolescence. He was in a place where I could no longer reach him; only the words of men had meaning for him then. He would be a mystery to me, a man, from that moment on.

Mothers are not alone in their sense of loss at such initiatory times. Children, indeed individuals of any age, experience this Mother-rift with every step away from dependence and irresponsibility. Can one choose consciousness, and in a sense leave home, without abandoning the unconscious matrix of one's being? Movement toward autonomy is often understood, in psyche, as a betrayal of Mother so acute it can strike her dead. The heroic journey begins as an act of infidelity, shrouded in ambivalence and guilt.

> Tiana, at twenty-five, lived in her parents' home, as did her two adult brothers. None had found a satisfying way to make a living. As Tiana approached the possibility of a good position in another city, she dreamt that her father had been unfaithful to her mother; he had betrayed her, and in the dream Tiana had felt torn between the two. In moving out into the world , in yielding to the forward thrust of her internalized Father, she was breaking faith with that inner Mother who needed to keep her children in the nest.[3]

Another woman could not consider marriage without dreaming of a mother's death.

> Upon her engagement Ellen visited her parents' Colorado ranch, only to find her ambivalence about the match renewed. When she returned to her fiance's city flat, she dreamt: "A woman, probably my mother, has died. I can see her upper body, her breasts, disintegrating as I watch."

With Ellen's wedding she would leave not just her family behind, but also the remembered paradise of her childhood home. The mountains had been Mother for her all her life; they would surely die without her love.

In "The Laidly Worm...," the fair mother/queen has died, grieving for her wandering son. The tale goes on:

> *The king mourned [his queen] long and faithfully, but one day while he was hunting he came across a lady of great beauty, and fell so much in love with her that he determined to marry her. So he sent word home that he was going to bring a new queen to Bamborough Castle.*

When the loving and containing mother dies, the way is open for a new queen, a Stepmother, to take her place. An obsessive yearning for the lost child may begin, sadness may become

---

[3]Throughout this book, the names of patients and others who've generously contributed their inner work have been changed to protect their privacy.

pathological despair, a sense of loss change to a refusal to let go. If a child is the only fullness in a woman's life, if her sense of self depends entirely on her ability to meet her child's needs, she may find she cannot set her child free.

> Fran, whose four-year-old daughter, Mindy, was referred for acute separation anxiety, mourned each of her child's birthdays and developmental milestones as the loss of her "baby", and as the loss of her own purpose in life. Far from being celebrational at such moments, she became angry, depressed and withdrawn, thus sending Mindy messages at odds with the child's natural desire for mastery. Not surprisingly, the child was developmentally delayed in a number of areas, but she was intuitively aware of the nature of her difficulties. Her first sandtray had a mother frantically digging through the sand in search of her lost babies. Her favorite story became that of Persephone and Demeter; she perceived her own struggle for autonomy as a separation from her mother's grief.[4]

Fran's need to keep her growing child a baby was related to her sense of emptiness, to the inner darkness she had suffered through for many years. She was so chronically depressed that only motherhood could sustain her life. On a subjective level, one can hardly find a more apt definition of depression than the departure of one's own youthful spirit. When this Childe Wynd sets sail, he takes all that is hopeful and exuberant with him, leaving darkness and despair in his place. That which is kind and nurturing within, one's own Good Mother, dies, to be

---

[4]Children often choose a tale, among the many that they see on my story shelf, to hear and hear again. In the abbreviated children's version of Mindy's favorite myth, Demeter was an earth goddess whose child, Persephone, wandered from her mother's side to gather up some flowers. When the girl pulled a narcissus from the earth she was carried off by Hades to his kingdom underground.

Demeter, in her rage and grief for her lost child, scoured the earth, letting it grow cold and fallow in her wake. The mother had no help from the other gods, but when men began to starve, Zeus, in his concern, sent Hermes to negotiate the girl's release. Because Persephone had eaten pomegranate seeds, the fruit of the dead, she was required to spend three months of each year in Hades' realm, reigning as his queen. She and her mother were reunited every spring.

replaced by a scolding, mocking Stepmother voice. The future gone, one is consumed by mourning for all that has been lost.

The dreams of a depressed woman reflected the loss of her youthful exuberance; a raging Stepmother possessed her life.

> Gloria, at thirty-eight, came into therapy full of despair. She found herself screaming at her two small sons and pushing her husband from their bed. She was unable to find any joy in work. Her dreams were fleeting, but those she could remember concerned a high school sweetheart, a wonderful young man who'd brightened her early life. In one such dream she felt that she'd lost him forever, and she could feel herself sobbing in her sleep.[5]

In our tale, the king finds his beautiful new queen while on a hunt. In bereavement of any sort, a search for the lost object may consume all the energy one has. Widows and widowers report scanning crowds for the face of the lost spouse; they find themselves approaching familiar figures on the street, only to turn away in tears when they realize their mistake. Movements are heard in the house late at night, doorknobs turning, footsteps in the hall. Shadows seem to move through rooms. Far from providing comfort, these elusive images disturb much-needed sleep, exacerbating emptiness too deep to bear.

The failed search constellates a raging fury, a fury that has the dead, abandoning partner as its true object but is likely to be displaced onto family and friends, onto those attempting to provide comfort, onto anyone not suffering one's fate. "Loss of a loved person gives rise not only to a cry for help but sometimes also to a rejection of those who respond...not only to an intense desire for reunion but to anger at his departure...." (Bowlby, 1980:31) The Stepmother, in all her witchy wrath, directs her darkness at all who might come near.

---

[5]As Gloria's work progressed, talented young men would come and go in her dreams. Their appearances ushered in a lifting of her spirits, times of high energy and creativity. Their departures were signals of depression in her outer life.

In agreeing to see a patient in the freshness of her grief, I made myself a target for a holocaust of rage:

> Helen had been in analysis for three years when her analyst became terminally ill. The nature of the illness had been taken up to some extent, but Helen was by no means prepared for the woman's rather sudden death. She blamed herself for having focused on the "trivialities" of her own life, for not having said an adequate goodbye, for not having been good enough to keep her analyst alive.
>
> She came to me for therapy immediately after the death, but she was terribly dissatisfied with me: I said things her analyst would have never said; I was poorly trained; I was neither old enough, large enough nor sufficiently detached; I was not the sort of person one could really trust. Moreover, her departed analyst, in a dream, had warned her against continuing with me.
>
> After six hours of work, having exhausted every possible opprobrium in describing me (while asking to see me at least three hours a week) she was finally clear on my greatest deficiency : I was not her dead analyst, nor could I ever be. With this, her anger left her, and another level of our work began.

I had the luxury of dealing with my patient one hour at a time; I could go off then and try to understand her need to tear me into shreds. In families, the Stepmother's rage is felt most painfully by those nearest to her fire, by children who can neither understand nor get away:

> Phil remembers his mother after his parents' divorce: She worked all day and he never knew what to expect when she came home at night. She would either be enraged, ready to pounce on Phil and his siblings at the smallest irritation, or she would withdraw into her room to cry, refusing to speak to them at all. They walked around her on tiptoe. Phil felt frightened, angry and often guilty, as if he should have been helping her in some undefined way.

The healthiest members of a family may generate the most anger; they are, at some level, blamed for their well being, the very sight of which offends Stepmother's eyes. Like Phil, such children can do no right, and must often swallow their own grief to accommodate the family's need. The "The Laidly Worm..." continues:

> *Princess Margaret was not very glad to hear of her mother's place being taken, but she did not repine...and at the appointed day came down to the castle gate with the keys all ready to hand over to her stepmother... "O welcome, father dear, to your halls and bowers, and welcome to you, my new mother, for all that's here is yours."*
>
> *So graceful and beautiful was Margaret that a Knight of the escort murmured admiringly, "Surely this Northern princess is the loveliest of her kind." At that the new queen flushed, and muttered below her breath: "I'll soon put an end to her beauty."*

In our story the Stepmother, unable to tolerate the saccharin sweetness of this child, immediately repairs to her dungeon to cast a spell. Margaret goes to sleep a princess, and wakes up an ugly, ravenous dragon. An illustration has the huge and scaly creature overflow her bed:

> *...[Margaret's] maidens ran away shrieking, and the Laidly Worm crawled and crept, and crept and crawled till it reached the Heugh, or rock, of the Spindleston, round which it coiled itself, and layed there basking with its terrible snout in the air.*

The black magic of a family's grief, however well hidden it may be, can indeed create an ugly worm where there had been a lovely, loving child. Bowlby (1980:121) writes of the effects of parental despair on family members:

> There can be little doubt that much of the disturbance reported in the surviving children is a result more of the behavior of the parents toward them than of any direct effect the death may have on the children themselves. Breakup of the marriage, mother's depression, explanations that God had taken the child who died can lead readily to anxiety...and to angry behavior.

Jung (CW 17:80-85), with more charity, spoke of such "spells" as the legacy of the parental unconscious. With no harm intended, much harm can be done.

> Children are so deeply involved in the psychological attitude of their parents that it is no wonder that most of the nervous disturbances of childhood can be traced back to a disturbed psychic atmosphere in the home...the things which have the most powerful effect upon children do not come from the conscious state of the parents but from their unconscious background...How are we to protect our children from ourselves...?

Jung, however, did not see the child's psyche as a *tabula rasa,* but as full of the collective wisdom of the ages, and very close to unmediated archetypal power (17:94-95). The projection of the powerful dragon is in keeping with a child's natural grandiosity, with his identification with that archetypal power. A child sees change in his environment, particularly emotional change in a caretaker, as a cataclysmic event for which he is somehow responsible: if he'd been a more obedient child, had had fewer angry thoughts, father (mother) would not have left (died, withdrawn); mother (father) would not be so unhappy, so angry, so distant. The child, in compensation for his actual powerlessness in the situation, imagines himself a Dragon, powerful enough to wreak havoc in the land, powerful enough to undo what has been done.

Allan, the eight-year-old son of a firefighter, "made up" this story shortly after his parents' divorce; his Dragon felt very powerful indeed:

> Once upon a time there was a fireman who decided to leave the firehouse because the kids in the neighborhood set too many fires and pulled too many false alarms. When they heard he was leaving the kids went to the firehouse and promised never to do these things again. The fireman thought about it and decided not to leave.

The boy clung to this fantasy, and worked at being very good for many years. His father, however, remarried soon after the divorce.

If good behavior fails, and it will surely fail, the smiling princess may indeed become a worm in a desperate effort to restore her happy home. If she can spit and roar and rouse the country round about, perhaps some help will come. Try as one might, one cannot hide so powerful a Worm behind the castle walls.

> Soon the country round about had reason to know of The Laidly Worm of Spindleston Heugh. For hunger drove the monster out from its cave and it used to devour everything it could come across.

Sally, a bright and once engaging child, was referred for pre-cipitously failing grades:

> Her parents had parted amicably, with an agreement for joint custody. A great deal of energy went into keeping the family peace, but the intuitive child sensed her mother's grief, her unspoken rage turned inward in barely contained despair. She also felt her father's growing distance from their life. Expressions of anger were so poorly tolerated in both households that the child was left to breathe her fire around the countryside: she bullied her classmates, torment-ed her teachers and was deliberately rude to neighbors. Both parents received reports and were forced to deal with one another as they dealt with her.

Kubler-Ross (1983:4) describes another dragon-child, the brother of a cancer victim who found himself virtually ignored by his grieving, angry parents:

> Billy started to injure himself weekly, but no one paid atten-tion to him....When he asked for a sandwich for lunch, his mother snapped at him, 'Can't you see I'm busy? Fix it your-self.' Billy started to wet his bed, and got a spanking for it. Later, a few months before his brother died, a teacher noticed that Billy was very cruel to a handicapped child

who attended school in a wheelchair. Billy later told Kubler-Ross, "Do you know I have asthma? But I guess that's not enough."

The Dragon Spell, burdensome as it is for the child, may serve to bring light into the darkness, for once the dragon is out and about the problems in the castle cannot be ignored. Where a woman may hesitate to ask for help for herself, for the raging Stepmother within, she may well seek help for her fire-breathing child. It is an axiom of family therapy that the "identified patient" speaks the family's truth. It is no less true that the disturbed child in treatment often brings a measure of healing to the family.[6]

The Dragon, in all its loathsomeness, carries Stepmother's darkness around it like a shroud. The dragon-child in a family, while carrying the family's grief, is the person most intimately connected to the Stepmother, the one best able to feel into her pain. In working with such children, one often finds great compassion just beneath their rage:

> A seven-year-old daughter of an alcoholic mother railed against her fate, and made life most difficult for everyone around her. She and her brother stayed with father in his mother's home, while their mother lived and drank alone. She often missed her visits with the children.
>
> In the girl's first sandtray a shark moved under water, devouring small, frightened creatures hiding in the corners. A scuba diver defended the creatures and attacked the shark. Mid-play, the child stopped and dripped red paint on the rubber shark. "I think it's wounded," she told me, with great sadness in her voice.

The countryfolk in our tale have heard the Dragon's roar; they go to a mighty warlock—one presumably in touch with the dark powers at play—for help and advice. He tells them:

[6]Were we to read this tale as subjective inner drama, we might see the Laidly Worm as a symptom too intrusive to ignore, a dream too ghastly to forget, a body pain that never goes away. The Dragon, as demanding as it is, is the pathology that leads one to a healing of the soul. (Cf. Hillman on "pathologizing".)

> *The Laidly Worm is really Princess Margaret, and it is*
> *hunger that drives her forth to do such deeds. Put aside for*
> *her seven kine, and each day as the sun goes down, carry*
> *every drop of milk they yield to the stone trough at the foot of*
> *Heugh, and the Laidly Worm will trouble the country no*
> *longer.*

The warlock has a message here for those of us concerned with the fire-breathing patients at our doors: However they've acquired their dragon skins, hunger has brought them, and hunger will not let them go. They must be fed and fed and fed, but with something more removed than mother's milk. If we can reliably deliver what is called for here—attention, interpretation, empathy—and then stand aside, the dragon will be free to feed itself.

Such patients often know precisely what they need. They demand attention but discourage all the therapist's attempts at warmth, at soothing mother love. They must be heard, but never taken to the breast.

> Nan, in her depression and rigidity, made every hour a
> struggle that left me completely drained. She presented
> dreams without affect or associations, then sat in stony
> silence, often refusing eye contact throughout the hour. She
> reminded me with some frequency that nothing had
> changed in her life except for those things which were so
> much worse since we had begun. She seemed so enraged
> that I wondered why she returned each week, except to
> pass her sense of helplessness along to me. I felt there was
> nothing I could say or do to ease her pain. When we began
> to plan around my vacation she broke down in tears, con-
> fessing in great anger that the hour was all that kept her
> going through the week; she was ashamed to feel such
> need, but my presence, apparently, was all that she
> required.

The Laidly Worm may feel contained and fed upon the Heugh, but for all of that, it remains a dragon still. If there is any hope of transformation, of freeing the Dragon from the

Stepmother's spell, it must come from somewhere beyond technique, beyond the egos of analyst and patient. The Warlock tells the countryfolk:

> But if ye would that she be [returned] to her natural shape…send over the seas for her brother, Childe Wynd.

The bereavement in this tale began with the departure of Childe Wynd; resolution of that grief depends on his return, on the spiritual renewal he represents, on the potential for wholeness that he brings. We look for his return in inner life, scanning the horizons for a puff of sail, but there is little we can do but wait and keep the harbor clear.

In our tale, Childe Wynd arrives in heroic splendor in a witch-proof ship, an army of loyal men at his side. The Stepmother, watching from her tower, perceives a threat to her very being. Childe Wynd's return could mean the end of her, an end to grief, and she must keep him far from home!

> [The Queen] summoned her familiar imps and said, "Childe Wynd is coming over the seas; he must never land. Raise storms, or bore the hull, but nohow must he touch the shore."

In abandoning one's grief, one might feel as traitorous as when one moves out into the world. Childe Wynd breaks faith with Mother when he leaves; he offends the Stepmother with his return. C. S. Lewis, in his memoir *A Grief Observed*, welcomed his own returning good spirits with considerable ambivalence:

> There's no denying that in some sense I "feel better," and with that comes a sort of shame, and a feeling that one is under a sort of obligation to cherish and foment and prolong one's unhappiness…. Every stile or clump of trees summoned me into a past kind of happiness, my pre-H. happiness. But the invitation seemed to me horrible….H. would die in me a second time; a worse bereavement than the first.

The Stepmother is not likely to let go without a fight. Her very being is a response to grief and she is not so easily dismissed when grief abates. For many patients every step toward health evokes a battle from within.

> Gloria's years of intensive inner work began to yield some fruit: she and her husband could enjoy moments of warmth and genuine intimacy, but not without a price. After a night of love she'd be wracked by violent body pains, as if a wrestling match were going on inside her thighs and lower legs. The battle, she felt, was between the old defenses that had served her well for forty years, and the openness she was just learning to enjoy. When the muscle spasms abated she felt bruised and battered from within; her "witchy one" had put up quite a fight.

Gloria's growing consciousness has sustained her through her pain; she comes to her inner battles well prepared. In our tale, Childe Wynd has also come ready for a fight:

> ...the imps went forth to meet Childe Wynd's ship, but when they got near, they found they had no power over the ship, for its keel was made of the rowan tree.[7] So back they came to the queen witch who knew not what to do....by her spells she caused the Laidly Worm to wait by the entrance of the harbor. As the ship came near, the Worm unfolded its coils, and, dipping into the sea, caught hold of the ship of Childe Wynd, and banged it off the shore.

The Stepmother, in her fear, sets sister and brother against one another; the Worm must fight to keep her brother's ship from land. In an illustration, the Dragon and the rescue ship struggle in the harbor, locked in entangled animosity. Like many sibling pairs engaged in lifelong war, they can neither separate nor embrace in love. Phil's dream is reminiscent of the embattled harbor scene:

---

[7]The Rowan is known for its power against fairies, sorcery and witchcraft in Scandinavian, Teutonic and Celtic mythologies (Cooper, 1978:142).

I am working in a hospital, on an acute care unit. One of the younger female patients is a particular problem. A nurse—my mother is a nurse—warns me to be careful around this patient; she is dangerous and may try to harm anyone who comes near her. I imagine the patient trying to slash me with a razor blade. When I come upon her in the hallway she tries to hit me with a mop handle, held out in front of her body. I disarm her and restrain her in my arms.

In working on this dream Phil recognized the girl as his younger sister, and found himself flooded with remorse. He'd fought with her throughout his adolescence, although she'd done little to provoke his attacks. He'd needed to take someone on, and he knew she'd never call for help; she'd feared their mother just as much as he.

It requires very little witchcraft to turn a brother and sister against one another in a spate of sibling rivalry. Any inequity will do, and no parent is capable of perfect equity in dealing with children.[8] The spell that has been cast in this tale is less about competition for the breast than about unconscious projection of parental fear and rage into the brother/sister relationship. The Worm and Childe Wynd fight one another at Stepmother's bidding, thus keeping her safely empowered. Brother/sister eros, with the intense empathy and intimacy it engenders, is the greatest threat to her existence; their battles keep her darkness alive.

A woman's life, given over to a grieving, internalized Stepmother, has been a case in point.

Carla's childhood was defined by her unhappy mother's dire warnings and cautionary tales, and at thirty-five she finds this dark, incorporated voice quite overpowering. She feels alone and terribly isolated, while fending off any

---

[8]Cf Mara Sidoli, "The Myth of Cain and Abel" for observations of sibling rivalry in early infancy. (*The Unfolding Self*, Boston, Sigo, 1989.)

opportunity for intimacy. Her closest male friend—a brother of sorts—has had similar difficulties, and their relationship has been one of long standing embattlement. She presents the following dream:

"I was leading Rob up a staircase; we were close. I told him he was just like family, and he embraced me. When I whispered that I loved him he became angry and withdrew; I called after him, saying that I loved him as a sister would. Later,—Rob leaves when his mother phones—his mother and mine are sitting in the dining room, complaining to one another about their lives. I sit with my eyes closed, my hands raised in prayer."

In a number of fairy tales, Stepmothers face defeat at the hands of loving brothers and sisters. "Hansel and Gretel," "Brother and Sister," and the "The Six Swans" come immediately to mind, but the imagery of "Fundevogel" best conveys the healing nature of the brother-sister bond. In this story a pair of foster children—father brings a foundling home as companion for his orphaned daughter—are united by their mutual bereavement; they pledge undying love and loyalty to one another. In their flight from the cook/stepmother/witch he becomes a rose bush, she a rose upon the bush; he a church, she a lamp in the church; he a pond, she a duck swimming in the pond. They outwit the witch together, in a way neither could alone.

Brother-sister relationships always carry the potential for intense intimacy. Who is closer, yet more mysterious, than one's opposite in the family? When the Good Mother has given way to her dark counterpart, when father is absent or abusive, child-eros unsuccessfully directed toward the parents flows most naturally to that intimate other. The bond that develops between brother and sister can be a saving grace, a bridge between infantile and adult libido, a healing container for wounded eros. This bond may live in psyche, in imaginal relation to anima/animus figures; it may be experienced with a natural brother/sister, or discovered in one "found" in outer life. In any case, the existence of such a mutually loving and protective relationship may be the greatest proof against the ravages and machinations of the Stepmother. The wholeness implicit in the incest bond is the antithesis of bereavement.[9]

The Stepmother's darkest spells, intended to split and separate brother and sister, may have the paradoxical effect of deepening their relationship. The witchcraft that keeps Childe Wynd from entering the harbor, from phallically acting out the love-bond with his sister, does not deter him. It only stirs his creativity.

> The incest prohibition acts as an obstacle and makes the creative fantasy inventive... In this way the libido becomes imperceptibly spiritualized. The power which 'always desires evil' thus creates spiritual life (Jung, 5:332).

In our story, Childe Wynd has been denied entry, his healing presence held at bay until he is forced into inventiveness. Straight-on heroics will not do here; he must retreat, make a lateral move, and approach the Dragon from an unexpected, unorthodox direction:

> *Then Childe Wynd ordered the ship to be put about, and the witch-queen thought he had given up the attempt. But instead of that, he only rounded the next point and landed safe and sound in Buddle Creek.*

The Prince's secret, sideways move is not unlike the left-handed greeting of the King and Queen in the *Rosarium Philosophorum,* an alchemical text:

> The gesture points to a closely guarded secret, to the "left-hand path," as the Indian Tantrists call their Shiva and Shakti worship. The left-hand (sinister) side is the dark, the unconscious side. The left is inauspicious and awkward; also, it is the side of the heart, from which comes not only love but all the evil thoughts connected with it, the moral contradictions in human nature that are expressed most clearly in our affective life (Jung, CW 16:410).

---

[9]I use incest here not in its pathological sense, but to indicate a strongly felt emotional union with a family member. This health-giving incest does not exclude erotic desire, but implies a containment of desire in imagination. Cf. Robert Stein, *Incest and Human Love* (Dallas, Spring, 1973) for expansion of this theme.

Childe Wynd, risking all the dark confusion of the approach from the heart, confronts his sister in her most frightening aspect.

> *[Childe Wynd], with sword drawn and bow bent, rushed up...to fight the terrible Worm that had kept him from landing.*

Despite all he's been told, he cannot believe that this Laidly Worm is the Princess Margaret; had she not kept him from the harbor, opposed him in a way his true sister would never have done? He draws his sword, prepared to slay the dragon, to kill soul just as she'd resisted spirit.[10] At this critical moment, Margaret speaks from the depths of her enchanted dragon heart:

> *Oh, quit your sword, unbend your bow,*
> *And give me kisses three;*
> *For though I am a poisonous worm,*
> *No harm I'll do to thee.*

Margaret, in naming the complex in which she is caught—perhaps she sees herself reflected in her brother's frightened eyes—finds her own voice within it. She is able to make herself heard above the Dragon-sound of antagonism and speak for eros. Thus, when she asks her brother to embrace the beast, as she has done herself, her voice rings with the authenticity born of recognition and responsibility. This voice, emanating from a fire-breathing Dragon's mouth, can move Dragon and listener alike:

> Erin, deeply embittered by the ending of a love affair, went on and on about her former lover's deficits and faults. After a time she paused, looked down, and was quiet for some time. When she looked at me again her face was softened

---

[10]James Hillman sees soul-danger in the Heroic Ego's swordsmanship: "...efforts to integrate, 'to bring these contents to light,' become a depotentiating of personifications and of their imaginal power, a drying up of the waters, and a slaying of the angel (seen to be a dangerous fairy demon by the ego), whose real purpose is to individualize itself....The Feminine image that the hero meets is his guardian angel, not his enemy, and it is her individualization...that matters to the soul." Cf. *Anima*, (Dallas: Spring, 1985:117).

by her tears. "You know," she said, "I think I'm not so easy to live with myself."

Childe Wynd, upon hearing his sister's voice, lays down his sword and listens; she speaks again:

> *O quit your sword, unbend your bow,*
> *And give me kisses three.*
> *If I'm not won ere set of sun,*
> *Won never shall I be.*

This is the moment of enantiodromia, of the eleventh-hour desperation that constellates its opposite. Margaret's life, the shape of her being, is at stake here; it is now or never. Her voice is so clear and strong in this moment that her brother can no longer deny her. Her consciousness of her own beastliness moves him through his fear and loathing, and he kisses the Dragon in all its ugliness. Like the kisses in "Snow White" and "Sleeping Beauty", these are kisses of redemption and rebirth. Childe Wynd serves as midwife to his sister's emergence from her dragon spell:

> *With a hiss and a roar the Laidly Worm reared back and before Childe Wynd stood his sister Margaret. He wrapped his cloak about her, and then went up to the castle with her.*

Brother and sister, together, have broken the Stepmother's dark spell; when this occurs in psyche the very air in the room seems to change:

> After a week's hiatus, Tiana looked very different. She'd had some sun, but the difference was more in her relaxed body posture, the smile that played around her mouth, the warmth in her eyes. Nothing had improved in her outer life; quite the contrary, but something had surely changed. Toward the end of the hour, she tentatively offered a dream: "I'm about to have incest with my brother..."

The Queen knows her hour has come; the kingdom's grief, at least for now, has been resolved.

Conclusion: An Unfinished Story

Childe Wynd enfolds Margaret in his cloak and they return together to the castle to confront the wicked Queen. Surprisingly, they make no move to kill her, but with the touch of a rowan twig return her to what must be her true shape, the shape of grief. She becomes a loathly toad, hopping and croaking about the castle grounds, a small, merely annoying version of the Dragon she'd cast upon Margaret (Jung, CW 14:25). The King is now free to rule his Kingdom once again, son and daughter by his side. But what are we to make of a quaternity that includes a toad?

In alchemical texts, the toad is paired with the soaring eagle, "which flies up to the clouds and receives the rays of the sun in his eyes":

> The toad 'is the opposite of air, it is the contrary element, namely earth, whereon alone it moves in slow steps, and does not trust itself to another element. Its head is very heavy and gazes at the earth. For this reason it denotes the philosophic earth, which cannot fly, as it is firm and solid. Upon it as a foundation the golden house is to be built. Were it not for the earth in our work the air would fly away, neither would the fire have its nourishment, nor the water its vessel (Jung, CW 14:2).

It would seem that the toad, with her heavy-headed, earthbound vision, has a necessary place in this royal family. The Stepmother's croaking voice, unpleasant as it may be, must continue to be heard in the castle grounds. She brings her dark weight to the airiness about her: to a king prone to enchantment by beautiful women, to a young, heroic prince, to a maidenly princess born afresh after a terrible ordeal.

Brother and sister are together now, but their union, healing as it has been, is not meant to last in this form forever. Childe

Wynd, still a prince after all, must continue his interrupted journey; Margaret may want to shed her brother's cloak and find one of her own. They must part with the familiar comfort of one another's arms and seek out strangers to bring new life into Bamborough Keep. The croaking toad, I suspect, will remind them of that task. She speaks for the dark necessities of nature, for leaving what is safe and known and taking one's chances in the world. While the Good Mother protects and enfolds, the Stepmother rejects her young, pushes them, protesting, out into the cold. The toad's continuing presence in the castle is to remind all of unfinished business.

Just so, the business of bereavement is never quite done. We are not meant to forget:

> The sorrow for the dead is the only sorrow from which we refuse to be divorced. Every other wound we seek to heal, every other affliction to forget; but this wound we consider it a duty to keep open; this affliction we cherish and brood over in solitude (W. Irving in Moffat, 1982:270).

Bereavement, with its memory of death, seems a requirement of soul. It is in the realm of Death, after all, that Psyche seeks her special beauty.[21] The Stepmother, as we've known her in this tale, serves to remind us of our grief, our losses and our little deaths. As toad, with her heavy, earthward gaze, she maintains a downcast, darkened view of life. In the face of "happily ever after", she remains:

> ...a loathsome toad is seen at times haunting the neighborhood of Bamborough Keep, and the wicked witch-queen is that Laidly Toad.

---

[21]Cf. both Neumann and Von Franz for their workings of the Psyche and Eros myth, in which Psyche must journey through the underworld before she can be reunited with her husband Eros. His mother, Aphrodite, requires the younger woman to fetch a box of beauty out of Hades' realm.

2

"Snow White" and the Loss of Youth
A Midwinter's Tale

This is what age must learn about:
The ABC of dying.
The going, yet not going,
The loving and leaving.
And the unbearable knowing and
knowing.

—E.B.White
Poems and Sketches

"*Once upon a time in the midst of winter....*" Thus begins "Snow White," a fairy tale we have come to associate with the young, developing feminine,[1] or as Jung would have it, with "the earth, held fast by winter's cold, awaiting the liberating sun of spring" (Jung 4, 496). When reading the story from this springtime perspective our tendency is to focus on growth more than decay, on resurrection more than on death, on life *in potentia* rather than on potency lost. The young heroine, carried off by the prince, transcends the dark powers personified by the evil queen, and all is well with the world.

---

[1]Bettelheim, in his classic analysis of "Snow White", states: "The fairy tale views the world and what happens in it not objectively, but from the perspective of the hero, who is always a person in development. Since the hearer identifies with Snow White, he sees all events through her eyes, and not through those of the Queen" (Bettelheim, 203).

If, however, we stay with the Stepmother's wintery perspective, within the barren landscape of loss, we read a very different story. "Snow White" becomes a tale of mid-life despair, of desperate attempts to escape the ravages of time, of obsessive, overpowering envy in the face of narcissistic bereavement. For the Stepmother/Queen, Snow White becomes an intolerable reminder of all that has been lost.

The Stepmother's tale, like Snow White's, speaks to development, to the feminine journey, but to the journey as descent. The Queen's movement is a movement toward death, and her kicking, screaming resistance is to the pull of gravity. She goes neither gently nor with grace.

> [Persons] at mid-life....enter a terrain that seems dark, unmarked, and lonely. For many it is truly a long dark night of the soul, a descent into regions of feeling and of experiencing that comes quite unexpected and certainly unsolicited. Midlife befalls us; we don't ask for it (M. Stein, 23).

We know, from a conventional reading of Snow White, that the Queen is the moving force behind her stepdaughter's journey. The reverse, I believe, is also true; it is Snow White's youthful presence that impels the Queen into her own dark terrain, into memory and a sense of loss. A patient had lived apart from her daughter for several years, but with the girl's return she was confronted with their differences, with her daughter's nubility and with her own lost innocence. She could remember her youth, but those days were long past recovery:

> Vivienne, at 40, sat in her kitchen and listened as her sixteen-year-old daughter returned from her junior prom. The girl and her date parked in front of the house and stayed there for quite some time, stirring Viv's imagination.
>
> As Vivienne fought the temptation to interrupt them—for perfectly sound parental reasons—she remembered her own convent school prom night, twenty-five years earlier. She'd been wearing a lovely red dress, she'd enjoyed the dance, but as her date tried to kiss her goodnight she'd turned away: "No! Sister says we mustn't!" Remembering, Viv

stayed in the kitchen that night, crying for all of her own missed chances.

"Snow White" speaks to the biological timetable that so often places adolescent girls in the care of crisis-bound mid-aged mothers, an irony of nature that may seem a poor practical joke to all concerned. Mothers and daughters find themselves caught in a maelstrom of mutual confusion and volatility, lost in the disorienting liminality in which both move. In the attempt to find shelter from the storm, to find a new, or renewed sense of identity, each may move toward rigid identification with one or another pole of an archetype: Senex *or* Puer, darkest black or snowy white, Stepmother or Stepchild. The confused ego-state of "has been and not yet,"[5] common to both adolescence *and* midlife, is split between them (Stein, 9).

In "Snow White", Stepmother and daughter force one another, respectively, out into life and back into reflection, this in the context of murderous envy and revenge. Each carries the other's opposite, each impels the other toward a healing of the split, toward a sense of wholeness.

The story, appropriately enough, begins as interior drama, before Snow White's birth, before any mother-daughter conflict. It begins in psyche, with a Queen and a wish:

> *Once upon a time, in the midst of winter, when the snow was falling softly from the sky, a queen sat by her ebony framed window sewing. When the Queen looked at the snow, she pricked her finger with the needle in her hand. Three drops of blood fell upon the snow, and she thought: "I wish I had a child as white as snow, as black as ebony, as red as blood upon the snow.*

The opening image is one of depression: a snowy landscape is framed in black, life seems suspended, frozen; winter appears to be endless, the cosmos caught in apparently permanent burnout. Within the depression, however, one can see small, barely discernible movements. A Queen, patient and quietly industrious, is sewing, perhaps making something new, perhaps mending a garment torn and frayed with age. It is a time for repair and restoration, for preparation, for the slow, tedious work that seems to be a part of winter's mood. The Queen's hands hardly ruffle the stillness, but she continues to sew in the cold light of the window. This is the quiet work of psyche, hardly noticeable but surely ongoing at those times when life is caught in midwinter darkness. While depression looks backward and rends its clothes in grief, The Good Queen prepares for whatever may come; she sews a trousseau, or a layette, and keeps the linens in good repair. There is no rush to the work—winter goes on for a very long time—but it does proceed, a stitch at a time.

The wish for a child interrupts this stillness with the immediacy of a pinprick, with the urgency of blood on snow. It is a bright new fantasy, the answer that will change everything, and change it forever. Framed in the desperation of depression, it carries within it both the passion of desire and the purity of the untried: black, red and white in lovely, irresistible combination.

The desire for a child, for new life, seems as inevitable a response to midwinter darkness as a solstice festival of lights; it is a longing for fresh possibilities, for the return of the light. Babies often appear in dreams of depressed patients, and can be understood as symbolically compensatory images of salvation, as manifestations of the archetypal Divine Child:

> ...the "child" paves the way for a future change of personality....[It is] a symbol which unites the opposites; a mediator, bringer of healing, that is, one who makes whole (Jung, 9i, 178).

Early in her analysis, Vivienne reported the following dream, in which the living child seemed a counterpoint to gray destruction, the beginning of new, green possibilities:

> There has been a nuclear war, and I am in a grey landscape, walking in a procession of dazed people. No color anywhere. I notice that I am carrying a swaddled baby in my arms; she's alive, I don't know if she's been irradiated,

but I hold her and keep going. Up ahead, very startling in the grey, is a green door, the only color in the dream. I go toward it, open it, and behind it is another green door, and another...

In some women the Child archetype, unacknowledged but active in the unconscious, may insist upon embodiment, manifesting itself in a series of "accidental" pregnancies that are later aborted in the face of practical reality. Or the desire for a baby may invade consciousness, become obsessional in its literality so that conceiving and bearing a child becomes life's sole object. In mother's imagination, biological child and Divine Child become one. The tale goes on,

> *When a short time had passed she indeed had a daughter whose skin was white as snow, whose cheeks were red as blood, whose hair was black as ebony. She called the little girl Snow White, and when the child was born, the Queen died.*

The difficulty comes with the reality of birth, with the human child and all of its messy, human demands. When the longed-for baby cries all night, when it fails, in its unrelenting neediness, to meet one's deepest needs, the Good Mother may indeed die, to be replaced by an impatient, angry, exhausted Stepmother:[2]

> The Grant's marriage counseling had gone quickly and well; they'd terminated with me mid-way through Mrs. Grant's welcomed pregnancy, feeling triumphant in the healing of their union through this new child. Eighteen months later, Mrs. Grant returned for individual work. She'd been terribly depressed since the birth of the child. It had been wonderful being pregnant, feeling her body working well for her, but the demands of mothering had raised a new set of

---

[2]Critics of the Grimm collection repeatedly remind us that Snow White's mother did not die a natural death; she was editorially murdered by Wilhelm Grimm. Grimm, in an effort to make the tale more palatable to parents and children, replaced the Good Queen with a Stepmother, thus preserving the "goodness" of the former. He nonetheless showed considerable wisdom and psychological sophistication in joining the Queen's death to the birth of her wish-child (Tatar, 24, 37, 143).

seemingly insurmountable problems. She hated the way she responded to her baby—she felt, in her anger and impatience, so much like her own mother—and memories of her own disturbed childhood were surfacing with alarming frequency.

Disappointment and despair may follow even when the wish-child takes other forms: the perfect job, the right man, a dream house, a newly svelte body, a completed degree, financial independence. It seems, at the moment of conception, that the wish, granted, will banish winter forever. In imagination, *in utero,* it is a beautiful, magical child. Again, the difficulty comes with birth. In the face of reality, fantasy dies; a wish granted loses its magical aura and brings unforeseen consequences in its wake.

> Barbara had joined a group, had worked with a nutritionist and diet counselor, and in a year's time had lost eighty pounds. She'd looked wonderful, felt more comfortable physically, but noticed that her husband was more distant than ever. In their twenty year marriage she'd been convinced that the chief impediment to their intimacy had been her excess weight. Having shed it, she was devastated by his negative response, and found herself responding, against her will, to the admiring glances of other men. A year later she began analysis, having regained most of the weight; she felt great loathing for herself and even greater rage toward her husband.

The disappointment, the sense of loss, that follows upon a granted wish seems to be one of the hallmarks of midlife, when success can be as painful, and as alien, as failure. Looking around at one's trophies, it's difficult to remember what the race was about. One asks: Who desired all of this? What has become of her?

> Kass at forty-five, recalls: "The last time I moved I left behind a huge, Spanish-style dresser, part of a bedroom set I'd bought ten years earlier. The piece was impressive, very expensive, and I'd wanted it with all my heart; I'd mounted a real campaign until I found a way to have it. But at mov-

ing time, when it was time to put it on the truck, it looked ridiculous, just too much wood, and I couldn't imagine ever having liked it. I left it there for the landlord."

When old furniture, old ways of wanting and being are left behind, there is a sense of dislocation, of alienation from a former self. The Good Queen, the patient, steady seamstress-by-the-window has died. In her wake comes a middle-aged woman caught in disorienting confusion. She is dissatisfied, without knowing why. Nothing seems to fit. Jung's description of the passage from childhood to youth suits her transition equally well:

> Something in us wishes to remain a child, to be unconscious, or, at most, conscious only of the ego; to reject everything strange, or else subject it to our own will; to do nothing, or else indulge our own craving for pleasure or power. In all this there is something of the inertia of matter; it is a persistence in the previous state whose range of consciousness is smaller, narrower and more egoistic than that of the dualistic phase. For here the individual is faced with the necessity of recognizing and accepting what is different and strange as part of his own life, as a kind of "also-I" (Jung 8, 764).

The inertia of matter takes hold of her soul. Caught in inner and outer changes beyond her conscious control, in the natural processes of aging, she resists these changes with all her being. In compensation for uncertainty, the New Queen, the Stepmother, becomes a woman given to vanity, to regressive, panicky clutching at familiar comforts. The desire to bear a Divine Child gives way to a desire to *be* that child. She enters the story bearing a mirror, a symbol of her narcissistic need.

> *A year later the King found himself another wife. She was beautiful but very proud, and most jealous of the beauty that was hers. She had a magic looking glass...*

The Queen trusts her mirror. It is absolutely reliable in its positive regard, reinforcing the childlike grandiosity with which she sustains herself.[3] The mirror, in an idealized (and idealizing) parental voice, tells her that she is not merely beautiful, but the fairest of all.[4] She may have suffered the disappointments and dislocations of midlife, but she is confirmed in her fantasy of having a special, unshared place in the sun. The mirror is her hold on life.

> It seems that the fear of loss of self (or soul) together with the attempt at retrieving the lost [self] makes the mirror so fascinating..." (Elkisch, 243)

There is something very familiar about this Stepmother Queen; we have all met her, in ourselves and in others. She is the prom queen who cannot give up her crown, the star athlete who will not retire, the straight "A" student whose world falls apart at the sight of a "B+"; she is, in her fantasy, her analyst's favorite patient, the one for whom he will surely break the rules. The Divine Child, the archetypically special one, is alive in all of us. Pathology lies in identification with its divinity, its entitlement. The Queen, caught in this grandiosity, might be the embodiment of the "Narcissistic Personality Disorder":

- [There is] an exaggerated sense of self importance [which] may be manifested as extreme self-centeredness and self-absorption.

- Individuals with this disorder are constantly seeking admiration and attention, and are more concerned with appearances than with substance.

- Self-esteem is often fragile, the individual may be preoccupied with how well he or she is doing and how well he or she is regarded by others. In response to criticism, defeat or disappointment, there [are] marked feelings of rage, inferiority, shame, humiliation, or emptiness.

---

[3] Cf. Kohut, Heinz: *The Analysis of the Self,* for a discussion of the "mirror transference" and its relationship to narcissistic need.

[4] Tatar (p.154) hears another sort of parental voice emanating from the mirror: "His [the father's] surely is the voice of the looking glass, the patriarchal voice of judgment that rules the Queen's—and every woman's—self evaluation."

- Entitlement, the expectation of special favors...is usually present.
- Interpersonal exploitiveness...for self-aggrandizement, is common; the personal integrity and rights of others are disregarded (DSM-III, 315).

For seven years, for the fullness of a cycle, the Queen is allowed her narcissistic fantasy. She remains the fairest in the land, buoyed by the reassurance of her magical mirror. We know nothing of her relationship with Snow White during this time; perhaps she sees the child as an extension of herself, as proof, in her perfect beauty, of her own perfection. Snow White, not perceived as separate from the Queen, may have served as another aspect of the mirror. This sort of mother-daughter identification, which seems to allow for nothing less than perfection in the daughter, may have life-long consequences:

> Laura, a strikingly beautiful young woman of 24, worried about spending a weekend visiting her mother. She had a miniscule blemish on her face and she was certain her mother would notice, and be terribly upset. In Laura's memory of her adolescence, the first signs of acne would send mother into panic-stricken consultations with dermatologists. Laura felt that her mother could not bear to look at her at these times. A year prior to the beginning of our work Laura had exposed herself to genital herpes, knowing that her partner was infected. In an unconscious effort to separate herself from and defy her mother—perhaps to protect herself from mother's envy—she had permanently blemished herself.

As long as Snow White is an extension of the Queen she cannot be her competitor, but their identity is not to last forever.

> ...Snow-White was growing more beautiful each year, and when she was seven years old she was more lovely than the Queen herself.

At seven, the child has reached "the age of reason," and she is well into the Oedipal age of acute sexual awareness. She is seen by the world, and sees herself, as a separate person. She is becoming herself, and in her becoming outshines her mother. This is a process fraught with terrible ambivalence for mother. Where pride has been, envy enters. Gloria remembers her mother's response to the bright, accomplished child that she was:

> I loved school and did very well. My mother responded to my "A"s, and to my musical talent, with warnings about modesty: "Don't get a big head," she told me. "People will resent you." When I grew tall and slender she called me a giant, and I began to slouch. When I entered Radcliffe she bragged about it to her friends, but made me feel a deserter for leaving home.

In "Snow White," the Queen cannot escape the sight of the beautiful child. To make things very much worse, she is informed by her wonderful truth-telling mirror of changes in her own persona. Does she see a grey hair, or the beginnings of lines around her eyes, her mouth? Is her fine, high color fading? She is still beautiful, true, but oh, that Snow White! *She* has a beauty untouched by time, unworried by life. The Queen's mirror tells her:

> *You, my Queen, are wondrous fair,*
> *But Snow White is fairer still.*

> *The Queen turned green with envy and with rage, and could not bear to have the child in her sight. Her hatred grew and grew, until she could no longer contain it in her breast.*

A scene from the 1986 movie, *Smooth Talk,* movingly illustrates a mother-daughter relationship gone sour with envy:

> Mother, not unattractive now and probably beautiful in her day, is dressed in a faded man's shirt. surrounded by the remains of breakfast in a messy kitchen. She looks tired and embittered. Her daughter, wearing a pink satin nightshirt, floats into the room. The girl seems to glow, to attract sunlight. She no sooner sits down than her mother begins to

berate her, to call her lazy, mindless and unfeeling. The girl is puzzled and wounded at the apparently unprovoked attack. She is only vaguely aware that her great sin lies in her untouched beauty.

"Snow White's" Queen does not deal with her envy in depressed withdrawal. She hides behind no old shirt, nor will she be satisfied with wounding words. She wants rid of this home-grown rival,[5] this thief of beauty, and she will do anything to regain what she has lost. Nothing less than a cannibal's feast will do. She calls for a huntsman, for one accustomed to the kill, and sends him off to return with Snow White's lungs and liver. What might she want here?

Lungs are containers for the *pneuma*, the spirit. Etymologically, "lung" is related to "light," in the sense of "without weight" (Haubrich, 141). How wonderful it would be to have the girl's lightness of spirit, to be without the weight of age! The liver is weightier stuff, but no less desirable:

> Plato said that the liver was a mirror on which the thoughts of the mind fell and were reflected as the image of the soul. The Odyssey calls the liver the seat of desire....By far,the most universal attribute of the liver...has been the belief that it is the seat of strength and courage (*Standard Dictionary of Folklore, Mythology and Legend, II,* 636).

The Queen is not content to merely kill the beautiful usurper; she wants to ingest her strength and vitality, her courage, her spirited lightness. The lungs and liver, stewed in salt, are to be a massive dose of Vitamin E, a preserved and preserving elixir of youth. For the Queen, this cannibalism is, in a sense, a religious act: to partake of Snow White is to be in communion with the Divine Child, to be one with perfect, untouched beauty.

---

[5]Cf. Bettelheim (194) for his thematic comparison of "Snow White" to the Oedipus cycle. Snow White's emergence as a threat at age seven certainly lends itself to an Oedipal interpretation, and following this line of thought Bettelheim sees mother's murderous rage as a projection of the child's desire to eliminate her as rival. He does not, however, preclude the possibility of envy in the heart of a mother.

The Queen is surely not unique in her appetite. The concretized desire to incorporate the young and beautiful is marketed in every health food store, at every cosmetics counter, in every boutique selling middle-aged women clothes designed for pre-pubescent bodies. Extracts of embryonic cells, imagined to have rejuvenating qualities, are sold at great cost to the credulous. Mothers, bereaved of their youth, borrow their daughters' clothes, hair styles and music, in the belief, perhaps, that they've borrowed their bodies, their lungs and livers, their endless adolescent energy. What is the cost to inner life of this manic search for youth?

> Forty-year-old Vivienne mourned the end of an erotic relationship by attending an all-night contra dance, spending hour after hour in the arms of energetic young men. Upon arriving home the next morning she fell into an exhausted sleep, and dreamt that the baby who'd been healthy and robust in recent dreams was ill, feverish, and greatly diminished in size. She thought (in the dream) "I've killed my child!" and ran to her mother for help.

Elissa Melamed, in her work on the fear of aging, reflects on the price of wrinkle-free skin:

> There is not too much you can do...except not move your face. This is seriously advocated in some circles....we are told to break those nasty habits like squinting and frowning. The very thought makes me scowl. I can see what it does to my face—but what would not moving my face do to my soul? (Melamed, 135)

Nonetheless, the Queen awaits the huntsman's return with her communion feast, with the bloody proof of her rival's death.

> *The huntsman took the child away, but when she began to weep he found he could not kill her after all. "Run away dear child," he said, then he stabbed a wild young boar that crossed his path, and took its lungs and liver to the Queen. Her cook salted them and served them to the Queen, and the evil woman thought she ate the lungs and liver of Snow White.*

The Queen's communion feast, as it turns out, is not of the Divine Child, but of another sort of god, the warlike boar. She takes in his fierce animal energy, a ferocity she will carry into her campaign against Snow White. The boar has his connection to the Goddess, but it seems to be to her dark, devouring aspect, to the Stepmother bent on destroying her young.[6] The Queen's envy is a wild boar on the loose within her. She consults her mirror, and she is once more confronted with the truth: for all her feasting, she has grown no younger.

> *Then she knew that the huntsman had lied; Snow-White was still alive! Her envy ate and ate at her, and she thought and thought again: how might she kill the child?*

Melanie Klein defines envy thus:

> ...envy is an oral-sadistic and anal-sadistic expression of destructive impulses, operative from the beginning of life....it has a constitutional [read: archetypal] basis....Envy is the angry feeling that another person possesses and enjoys something desirable—the envious impulse being to take it away or spoil it....The envious man sickens at the sight of enjoyment. He is easy only in the misery of others....It could be said that the very envious person is insatiable, he can never be satisfied because his envy stems from within...(Klein, 176).

The Queen is terribly victimized by her envy, it is a raging monster tormenting her from within, allowing her no rest. Snow White has found solace, shelter and protection with the seven dwarfs but the Queen has no confidant, no one with whom to share her darkness. She finds no comfort in the mirror—the demon is not pretty—nor protection from her inner storm. A

---

[6]The boar is "intrepidity, lust, gluttony; prophesy, magic, warfare...destruction and strife...an attribute of Demeter and Atalanta; a storm animal; funerary; sacred to Woden/Odin (Cooper, 22).
  "Vishnu the Boar represented an early attempt to reassign to a male body the holy creative blood of life, the Goddess's menstruum....he was worshiped in conjunction with the Goddess by Germanic Aryans...." (Walker, 112).

patient experiences this envy as a "witch" who comes and goes at will:

> Gloria's intensive work around her own childhood seems to evoke an inner Stepmother who possesses her for hours at a time; she finds herself envying her children their good parenting; they don't have to suffer as she has done, and there are times when this feels unforgivable. "I woke up feeling witchy, screaming at the boys for nothing, but I just couldn't stop myself. I hated my children for not having to live my childhood, but here I was sounding just like my mother, maybe worse than she ever had. I looked in the mirror and saw this terrible woman there, and couldn't look again. The part of me that could stand aside and watch wondered if I was doing the boys irreparable harm, but the thought made me even angrier."

"Snow White's" Queen, completely caught up in her envy, uses all her creativity in its service. She sets aside her regal persona, no comfort to her now, and dresses like a peddler. It is a costume more syntonic, perhaps, with her sense of deprivation. Finding Snow White in the cottage beyond the seven hills—such a great distance from the castle!—she appeals to her vanity, (and perhaps to her need for mothering) and sells her some pretty laces for her bodice.

> *"My child, what a wreck you are! Come here, let me lace you properly for once." Snow White, having no suspicion, let the woman tie the laces round and round.*

Age will always envy youth her unbound spirit, will always need to leaden her lightness with suspicion. The Queen's need to bind Snow White, to constrict her free-breathing innocence, is Senex's response to the Puer:

> Let us look at the usual recommendations for the "first-half" of life, or "how to cure a puer:" analyze the unconscious, reduce the fantasies, dry the hysterics, confront the intuitions, bring down to earth and reality, turn the poetry into prose...the provisional [is to be] overcome through the

panacea of commitment....Note well: All these images are Saturnian (Hillman 1979, 28).

I recall a family party some years ago, a time of sweet initiation for my daughter. The warning I received that night, as I hear it now, was as much about the Queen as about Snow White. My mother was telling me about Stepmotherhood:

> The patio was set up as a dance floor, and my daughter, wearing her first long dress and looking very beautiful, wanted to dance. She was almost twelve. I encouraged her to go to it, and she was soon dancing with her cousin and his friends, looking absolutely, radiantly happy. Aunts and uncles stood with me to watch; it was a lovely sight. Then my mother approached me, shaking her head in my daughter's direction. "You'd better watch her!" she said. "That one will be trouble."

Youthful beauty, when touched by Eros, is indeed troublesome to the eyes of experience. At such times envy, the wish to bespoil the pleasure of the other, takes the form of parental protectiveness, of age's duty to the young. In Apuleius' tale of Psyche and Eros, Psyche's parents, perceiving their own envy in the envy of the gods, consult Apollo's oracle. The news they receive, an Apollonian judgment of immoderate Eros, confirms their worst fears for their daughter:

> Nor hope a son-in-law of mortal birth, But a dire mischief, viperous and fierce, who flies through aether and with fire and sword, tires and debilitates all things that are...(Graves, 100)

When envy-as-protection is at play, Eros will always seem monstrous, his arrows lethal. Psyche's parents, knowing something of the nature of love's abyss, and regretting their knowledge, see their daughter's leap as a movement toward death. Their wish is to protect her, to bind her to them forever. The envious Queen can find all sorts of sound, protective reasons for locking out Eros, for tugging on those bodice-laces. There are, after all, drugs in the schools, muggers on the streets, and lechery in the hearts of all young men. In the name of good parenting the Stepmother restricts opportunity, withholds information, and ties daughter close to her with pretties, with material rewards for good, *i.e.* sexually constricted, behavior. In our story, Snow White buys the laces and stands still for the binding. This Snow White may be frightened, uneasy with her growing body and with the power of its sexuality. I have seen her in adolescents who somehow leave their diaries, their repositories of sexual fantasy, in mother's path. Snow White is calling for the Stepmother, unconsciously taunting her with the richness of unbound imagination. When the Queen hears the call and responds in her predictable way, the girl is properly outraged at the invasion of her privacy; she may also be relieved by the restrictions that follow.

> *[The old woman] tied so quickly and so tightly that the child lost her breath and fell down where she stood. The Queen, certain now that Snow White was truly dead, thought, "Now I am the fairest in the land," and ran away.*

The Queen, at her most dangerous as internalized demon, may play a major role in an anorexic's progress toward death. She offers a promise of beauty in the silken laces, and holds herself up as mirror, a mirror which only reflects perfection and its loss. If one is not the Most Beautiful, one is nothing. The Queen lives this philosophy and Snow White, lacking her own truthtelling mirror, takes it in as truth. She allows the Queen to tie her tiny bodice ever tighter, to bind off any hint of breast, any sign of fleshy femininity. The "proper lacing" can be lethal; the girl's life hangs on the timely appearance of the Dwarfs:

> *When they lifted her and saw the bodice laces tied so tight, they quickly cut her free. She soon began to breathe once more.*

Much has been made of these seven little men:

> ...one critic tells us that the dwarves in "Snow White" should be viewed as siblings of the heroine, another asserts

that they represent the unconscious, and a third declares them to be symbols of creative activity...(Tatar, 54).

They may be all of the above, but their function in the story is clear: they keep Snow White alive and ground her in the business of everyday living. Salvation lies in simple practicalities.

> Kate's dream heralded the end of a long, suicidal depression: "The world was about to end in a nuclear explosion. In anticipation of this, people were lined up for cups of poison. I could see my sister, ahead of me in line, drink hers. Then I saw a spaceship land, and watched some very small men emerge from the ship. I knew they would solve the problem, knew that I wouldn't have to die. I left the line and started toward home, one of my children on each hip. When I arrived home the small people were waiting for me on my front step, expecting something of me. I took them to the kitchen and made them some tea."

Far from offering Snow White free board, the dwarfs have their own demands and restrictions, their own senexy response to youth:

> *If you cook for us and clean our house, if you will wash, sew, and knit and make the beds, then you may stay with us. You shall have all you need as long as you are here.*

They keep Snow White busy and, as long as she's alive, well off the pedestal. The Stepmother despises the girl's snowy whiteness; the dwarfs ask her to transcend it. The Queen lives as if beauty were all; the dwarfs, while enjoying the girl's beauty, expect her to wash the dishes. The Queen wants the lovely young thing to die; the dwarfs tell her to grow up. They work against the Queen's dark magic with their demands for competence, thus cutting the mother-ties of dependency that might bind Snow White to a permanent childhood.

> Ellie at eight made terrible messes in my playroom for the simple pleasure of cleaning up at the end of the hour. Her mother was invested, to some degree, in keeping her bound up in dependency, but she'd promised her the chore of dry-

ing dishes as soon as she'd turned nine. Ellie couldn't wait that long. Being helpful meant growing up.

The Queen, returning to the castle, once more consults her mirror, once more receives the terrible news: Snow White is still alive!

When she heard that, she was filled with fear....

The Queen's desperation grows. It will take more than pretty laces and quick fingers, more than restrictions and constrictions to kill the snow white naiveté that taunts her so. The very thought of the girl ages her! I recall a recent analytic session in which my senexy response to New Age psychology met my envy of unfettered youth:

> Sara came in absolutely glowing with the effects of a weekend workshop she'd attended on an island off the coast. She had, she felt, been enlightened and empowered; issues we'd worked on for months had been resolved. She was thinking about taking a four-week version of the workshop, to be staged on a river rafting trip, later in the summer.

I could feel myself growing older as she spoke. Nothing so quick and easy could be real! Psyche, I thought, requires pain, and years of darkness, before she yields her wisdom. And how could Sara spare four weeks to go rafting down a river? When she'd stopped, and was clearly waiting for my response, I wanted to tell her it was nonsense, tell her it was time to settle down and get to work. Instead, and after some reflection, I confessed that I envied her her freedom and enthusiasm. She'd clearly had a wonderful experience.

The Queen's mirror, alas, does not seem made for freeing self-reflection. Caught in her envious response to Snow White's innocence, the Queen turns to witchcraft and makes a poisonous comb, just the thing for taming Snow White's crowning glory.

Hair is "the life force; strength; energy; the power of thought, inspiration; hair flowing loose depicts freedom, the nubile state; bound, it is...subjection (Cooper, 77). "The ancients insisted that women needed their hair to work magic spells; thus women deprived of their hair were harmless... (Walker, 368). How does one use a comb—that "attribute of Venus, sirens and mermaids" (Cooper, 42), without poisoning its use? How might any Queen tame Snow White's sensuality, her free-flowing nubility, without spoiling it and somehow curtailing her feminine energy? From the parental perspective, the girl's naiveté, her incredible lack of suspicion, is terribly dangerous. Her lovely, unbound hair *needs* the comb!

As a young therapist I found mothers of adolescent girls unduly paranoid, fearing their daughters' pregnancies, accusing the girls of lascivious thoughts they'd surely never had. Then, when my daughter was fourteen, I had a dream which brought me face-to-face with the archetypal nature of this fear. I dreamt:

> My daughter was pregnant. She'd been tested at the Health Center [where I worked] and a nurse had called to tell me that the test was positive. I called my daughter with this news, but she could not take in the import of the tragedy. She said, "Positive is good, isn't it? Why are you upset?" Her naiveté enraged me. I woke thinking that the dream was nonsense. My daughter wasn't even dating, was she? Still, I could not get back to sleep, the terror and frustration of the dream stayed with me. Knowing full well I was caught in irrationality, I got up and checked her box of sanitary pads. To my great relief, the new package had been opened; I was able to return to sleep, with a sense of initiation into the panicked ranks of adolescents' mothers.

The world can be a dangerous place for the young and innocent, and children now are routinely and publicly cautioned about unwelcome touch, about seduction by strangers, about pregnancy and AIDS. The Stepmother enters when protectiveness meets envy, when snow-whiteness becomes a goad, an unwelcome reminder of one's darkness. The comb then becomes a witch's tool, steeped in the poison of bitter experience. Its purpose is not so much to inform innocence as to kill it altogether.

Snow White had no suspicion, but as soon as the comb had touched her raven hair the poison took effect, and she fell senseless where she stood.

At the touch of the comb Snow White's senses are numbed, her sensuality neutralized, her sense of herself in relation to others thoroughly poisoned:

> Carla, at thirty-five, might be the model for Snow White. She has the pristine beauty of a young girl, as if she'd spent twenty years packed in cotton or encased in a glass coffin. As a child she was warned against the dark intent of strangers; more, against the mediterranean warmth of her father's family. Adolescence brought more warnings, couched in the most frightening terms: any venture away from home was seen as an invitation to rape. Sexuality, she was told, was simply a lure into marriage, viewed by both parents as a kind of death. As an adult, Carla has thoroughly internalized the poison; she is her own Stepmother. She views all friendship with suspicion, all need for human contact as weakness, any hint of intimacy as manipulation. The center of her sandtray work is often a frozen lake.

The problem of the comb is surely not confined to parents and children, but comes up unavoidably in analysis. How do we offer the comb, as an instrument of consciousness, while keeping it free of the poison of our envy? Men and women of any age may bring Snow White into the room, in all her untouched innocence, as a new love affair, a wonderful idea, an experience glowing with numinosity. In response to the radiance of this Divine Child, and in the name of consciousness, we begin a search for shadow, for some way to bind the wild optimism of the patient's attitude. Can we comb without killing?

> Kate remembers telling a former analyst about the start of a new love affair: "We'd met through the personals and he just swept me off my feet with his wonderfully romantic gestures. I was forty years old, but this was all new for me. When I told Y. his first response was, "You know, of course, that he's married." I didn't know, or didn't yet

know, and I surely didn't want to know just then. His remark kept me from seeing the real situation for quite some time. I just couldn't let him be right.

It may be no accident that the analyst is sometimes imagined as barber, or hairdresser:

> When...the analyst is represented as a hairdresser (because he "fixes the head") the analyst is being not so much disguised as devalued. The patient, in her conscious life, is only too ready to acknowledge any kind of authority....The analyst, says the dream, should have no more significance than the hairdresser who puts her head right so that she can then use it herself (Jung 13, 479).

It may be that Snow White is more in need of a well-polished mirror than a comb. I can remember reporting a most numinous dream, just basking in the glow of it. My analyst smiled, and remarked that we could surely end the analysis now; what more could I possibly require? His reflection of my euphoria was all that I needed to bring me back to earth.

In our story, the life-giving dwarfs free Snow White from the effects of the poisonous comb; she lets her hair down and proceeds with her chores, perhaps with a bit more caution. The magical mirror so informs the Queen:

> *With this, the Queen was overcome with rage. "Snow White must die," she screamed, "even if I die myself!"*

Melamed, in *Mirror, Mirror,* reports that women electing cosmetic surgery tend to disregard all warnings about the risks of such surgery: paralysis, nerve damage, hemorrhage, the difficulties of general anesthesia. It is worth their lives to have a new face, a sculpted body—to be the fairest in the land.

These women reported some of their motivations for surgery:

> Hope that the operation would make them feel physically younger; desire for involvement with younger people,

desire for sexual freedom; to get a better job, to cure husband's impotence, to compete with a sixteen-year-old
daughter... (Melamed, 143)

"Snow White"'s Queen has no wizard/surgeon ready to alter
reality, and her mirror is unrelentingly honest; there is nothing she can do to turn back time. In her great desperation
she is driven inward, and she feels the bright and youthful girl
within begin to die. She removes herself to dark, suicidal
contemplation:

> *She closed herself into a dark and secret room, a lonely place
> where no one ever came, and fashioned there a beautiful
> and lethal fruit.*

The Queen cannot steal Snow White's perfect beauty, but she
can surely spoil it. The apple, so tempting that all would want a
bite, has a long history as a spoiler; it is the forbidden fruit of
knowledge, Eris' apple of discord. At its center is a distillate of
the Queen's own poison, all of her unworked, or overworked,
unhappiness, all the bitterness and disappointment of a lifetime
concentrated into a deadly essence.

Marilyn French, in her novel *Her Mother's Daughter,* writes
movingly of the poisoned apple. The protagonist describes her
mother, ruminating on the pain of her early life:

> ...it is her enduring truth and nothing that has happened
> since has touched it. Her sorrow is the one thing she trusts,
> her jewel, her truth; it is the pearl she has created out of her
> wretchedness, the one thing she owns, the one thing that is
> indisputably hers (French, 66).

The Queen, dressed in her peasant rags, offers a (finally!)
wary Snow White the beautifully polished apple:

> *"Do you think I'd poison you?" said the Queen. "Here, I'll cut
> the fruit in half; I'll eat the white cheek, and you can have
> the red."...Reassured, [Snow White] reached out for the lovely
> fruit, but hardly had it in her mouth before she fell down
> where she stood.*

The Queen and Snow White each have their bite of the apple. As is the case in French's dark novel, the poison is to be shared, to be passed from mother, who has immunized herself with use, to daughter, for whom the poison is lethal in its red intensity. They cannot share pleasure and success; there is too much envy for that. Only pain can bind them together.

> [Mother's sorrow is] cruel, cruel to us who love her, who have tried....Bad, selfish, cruel, yet I understand it, I am just like her, I am being transformed into her, clutching *my* pearl of inconsolability...Her life wasn't mine. But I drank hers in, I made it my own, trying to lift its burden from her (French, 660).

Snow White tastes the fruit, and falls down dead. The poison is so lethal one need not swallow it, need not consciously believe in it, to suffer its effects. Nor do mothers consciously wish their pain on their daughters; it is the Stepmother, the dark, unconscious one, who passes on the fruit of her woundedness.

> What usually has the strongest psychic effect on the child is the life which the parents have not lived...[that is,]that part of their lives which *might have been* lived....One should never forget that it is a question of "original sin," a sin against life and not a contravention of manmade morality....we seem to be dealing with some fate-like ethos beyond the reach of our conscious judgement (Jung 17, 88).

All of the good care of the dwarfs cannot bring Snow White back to life; her untouched innocence is no longer, her purity has been fatally sullied by the Stepmother's dark potion. The little men prepare a vessel for her long incubation, a glass coffin in which the apple-poison can become its own antidote and death can prepare for rebirth. When Eros jolts the King's daughter back into life she is ready for him; the lonely, enclosed time of waiting has been a passage from which she emerges a woman, open to relationship.

The Queen, too, has had her quiet time. With Snow White's death her torture is abated:

[Then] her rageful heart had rest....

Snow White's time of transformation may also be a time of reflection for the Queen, a time for reassessment. Freed of her daughter's blinding whiteness, and of the demonic power of Stepmother envy, perhaps she sees herself in a clearer, softer light. Can she admire the drama of her silvered hair, can she feel a fascination with her well-lined face? In her own land, she is indeed fair. In her envy of Snow White she'd been the youth cult's most fervent devotee; that devotion clouded her mirror. She has time now, and opportunity, for a new vision of herself.

> The process of aging is a great lightening up of false tensions that come from romance, from having certain ideas of yourself, and from things you think you have to have....It is a slow process of undoing all the knots. And it takes courage to leave the security that youth, sex and the passport of attractiveness bring. But Life is kind. It gives you time (Melamed, 205).

The Queen's peace is interrupted by an invitation to Snow White's wedding, this followed by some very bad news. Her mirror tells her:

> *"My, Queen, you are the fairest here,*
> *But the new young Queen is by far more fair."*
>
> *Then the Queen swore and cried and moaned in utter misery. What was she to do?*

The wedding stirs all of the Queen's sleeping demons, as weddings often will. A bride is indeed a young queen, meant to be the center of attention, to outshine every other woman in the room. The mother-of-the-bride must not only stand in her daughter's shadow but face her own losses on every level; her relationship with her daughter will never be the same; the young woman will have her own, separate life. Worse, the bride's joyful optimism, her bright white hope, raises the memory of each of her mother's life disappointments. The Stepmother's envy, deep-

ened by her sense of bereavement, may move her to darken the
wedding day with dire warnings and cautionary tales:

> Zoe's parents were divorced shortly after her birth, and
> Zoe's mother raised her alone, making the girl the center of
> her life. When Zoe, at twenty-four, decided to marry, her
> mother shocked her with a series of letters berating the
> young man and predicting a life of misery should she stay
> with her choice. The couple nonetheless planned a family
> wedding. Zoe's mother attended, but in such a clear state of
> grief that a dark pall was cast on the occasion.

Traditional Jewish weddings seemed to take in mother's grief,
her sense of displacement, and offered her honor as an antidote
to Stepmother darkness. The last child in a family to marry,
whether bride or groom, would join his or her siblings in crowning their mother with a wreath of flowers. They would then circle the seated woman in a dance, honoring her as the true
queen of the evening. She'd fulfilled her mother-role and prepared her children for the future, for their lives as husbands,
wives and parents. The floral crown seemed to speak to completion, to the end of a life-phase. Both mother *and* children were
about to cross a threshold.

Snow White, however, is bent more on revenge than on
bestowing honor. No longer so sweet and innocent, she seems
to have taken in some Stepmother darkness as she invites the
unwilling Queen into another sort of dance:

> *Snow White…was expecting her. Iron dancing shoes had
> been set upon the fire; they were brought to the wicked
> Queen with tongs. She was forced to dance in the red-hot
> shoes, and dance she did until she died.*

Jung (9i, 352) associates dance with transformation and with
the necessary death of Maidens, "because their exclusive domi-
nation of the feminine psyche hinders the individuation process,
that is, the maturation of personality." Snow White, in her vengeful act of ordering the dance, turns up the heat and outdoes the
Queen in her sadistic creativity. She acts out the death of her

maiden purity, and she'll no longer need the Queen to darken her shining whiteness. She has, in a sense, done her own dance of death. Now it is time for the Stepmother to die.

Until this point in the story the positive and negative aspects of the feminine have been split between the two figures. The tortured death of the Stepmother, of her demonic, archetypal envy, follows inevitably the death of Snow White's perfect innocence and goodness. There is nothing in this story's end of happily-ever-after for the bride and groom. The Stepmother's death, completes the tale.

Conclusion

If we could read beyond the tale's end we might see that the archetypal split has been healed, that having joined one another in a wedding dance, in the body's celebration of union and wholeness, mother and daughter have emerged as individuals, neither Good nor Bad, Young nor Old, but women joined in their humanity.[7] Both have been freed from the gripping power of the archetype. A mother who can dance at her daughter's wedding, who can celebrate this passage in the girl's life, and in her own, is no longer caught in the Stepmother's bitter envy. The Old Queen is dead.

The colors of this tale, virginal white, deadly black, and passionate red have been played out in all of their opposition, and in all of their unity. The Queen, in blackening her daughter's whiteness, in feeding her the poisoned fruit of knowledge, has readied her, in her way, for life in the world. By the end of the tale the snow-white princess has become a young queen, with a growing sense of her own power.

The Stepmother, on the other hand, has been moved by Snow White's untouched innocence, by her affronting whiteness, into a new sort of reflection, into the "secret, lonely room," where

---

[7]Jung found an association between dance and the Mandala, a symbol of wholeness and of the union of opposites. "Among my patients I have come across women who did not draw mandalas but danced them instead....[The patients] find that [the dances] somehow express and have an effect on their subjective psychic state" (Jung, 13,32).

her blackest passions are reflected in the mirror: envy, murderous rage, suicidal despair. Her attempts to cling to youthful beauty and to her childlike fantasies of specialness, fail repeatedly. She must learn to live with her aging body and her imperfect soul. Like Snow White, she must let go of her maidenly perfection, accept degeneration and decay, and in doing so, embrace her wholeness. This slow acceptance is a forced and tortured wedding dance, a rite of death, union and renewal. She marries Shadow, and the possibility of death. The rebirth of the Queen is not in the fairy tale; it is in her suffering, her dark reflections, her joining her daughter, however painfully, in celebration of their lives as women. She dances neither gladly nor with grace, but dance she does. The persona-bound, narcissistic one dies, as she must, but a newly conscious woman may be born.

3

"HANSEL AND GRETEL"
AND THE IMPOVERISHED STEPMOTHER

...the folk fairy tale conveys an important, although
unpleasant truth: poverty and deprivation do not improve
man's character, but rather make him more selfish, less sen-
sitive to the sufferings of others, and thus prone to embark
on evil deeds.

—Bruno Bettelheim
The Uses of Enchantment

Once, on the edge of a great forest, there lived a poor wood-
cutter, his two children and his wife. His son was called
Hansel, and his daughter, Gretel.

For many years, a large part of my therapeutic work was
with poor, abused and neglected children. "Hansel and
Gretel" was their favorite story. More than any other familiar
tale, this story spoke to their reality: to the impoverishment of
soul and spirit that comes with hunger, to the constant fear of
abandonment and loss that seems to be a part of poverty, to
the price to be paid in eros for day-to-day survival. In the fairy
tale, Hansel and Gretel live through deprivation, abandonment
and the terrible discovery that candy-coated sweetness can

contain the Witch. Still, they overcome. The Good Mother is never personified in this tale, not even as a figure in memory, but she seems ever present as an inner resource. Hansel and Gretel have the capacity to find comfort and guidance in the brightly shining moon, in a God who will not forsake them, in winged guides and couriers. They live "hard by a great forest," close to nature, close to the unconscious. Therein lies their strength.

But this is more than a story of survival. "Hansel and Gretel" touches on the most primitive and basic of human relationships, that of the hungry, helpless (and/or sadistically aggressive) infant and his rejecting (and/or devouring) mother. The tale raises complex, perhaps unanswerable questions: How do mother and child feed, and feed upon, one another? How do conditions of emotional and material poverty affect mother and child separately, and in relationship to one another? In the absence of "good mothering," how does a child grow?

This tale is rich in Dark Mothers; we are given the cold-hearted woodcutter's wife *and* the child-eating Gingerbread Witch. Taken together they are the worst of Stepmothers, rejecting and withholding on one hand, sweetly devouring on the other. Both are beset by loss. We meet the former in her depletion; she is starving, and consequently dry of the milk of human kindness. The latter is betrayed by the apparent abundance of her breast, by her temptingly sweet persona; the children eat her out of house and home. The Stepmother and the Witch are mirror images of one another, each a reflection of and a response to the other's experience. They exist side-by-side, each a part of the other, and both in relation to hungry, needy, greedy children. They do not enter this tale to replace a Good Mother who has died; in one form or another, they have always been part of the story, a part of the milieu of poverty.

"Hansel and Gretel" begins with a statement of collective and personal poverty. A poor man, the father in this tale, is at the end of his rope. Things were never good for him; in a time of general famine he finds himself entirely depleted, without hope, without a plan. The tale opens with his insomniac despair:

They had little enough in the best of times, and when a great famine struck the land, they could find no means to buy their daily bread. When night fell it brought the woodsman little rest, only worry of the day to come. "What are we to do?" he groaned to his wife: "How are we to feed our children when we have nothing for ourselves?"

His wife, soon identified as the children's Stepmother, quickly becomes the villain in the piece. Faced with starvation and with her husband's helplessness, she does make a plan, but one not likely to elicit sympathy:

"Husband, hear me well," she said, "tomorrow we will take the children to the deepest woods, give them each a piece of bread and light a fire. We will leave them there, go about our work and not return. They'll never find their way back home, and we shall be rid of them for good."

This Stepmother will not be the self-sacrificing, all-giving mother of romanticized poverty. She has been reduced by destitution to her darkest instinctuality and she'll abandon her children as a matter of survival; it is her life or theirs. When her husband balks at her plan she quiets him thus:

"...prepare our coffins then, for soon we'll all have starved."

The wood-cutter's wife has nothing more to give; she believes that her children will destroy her, devour her in their neediness. She might well subscribe to the Kleinian vision of the child as an innately sadistic, murderous being:

[The child] has certain oral-sadistic phantasies of a quite definite character...in which he gets possession of the contents of his mother's breast by sucking and scooping it out. This desire to suck and scoop out, first directed to her breast, soon extends to the inside of her body...[the child's] predominant wish is to rob her body of its contents and destroy it (Klein 1960, 185).

This devouring infant seems the polar opposite of the Divine Child, a symbol of death and fragmentation rather than of wholeness and new life. This image of the child-as-cannibal would have great resonance for the Stepmother as we have defined her, for a woman bowed with bereavement, with destitution.

How might a child look, for instance, to an overburdened, adolescent mother, alone and still childlike in her need for mothering? Her infant's most instinctual move might be perceived as an attack upon her meager resources. A worker in an early intervention program told the following story. Her client was twenty; the newborn baby was the client's third:

> She was all alone when I arrived for the home visit, and in labor; her boyfriend had cut and run the week before. We left the kids with a neighbor, and when I drove her to the hospital, she begged me to stay with her. The labor went quickly, it was over in three hours, and she was awake at the end. The baby looked healthy and beautiful, and when they gave her to her mom she reached out her little arms for her, but the mother pulled right back. "Look at that," she said to me, "a few minutes old and she's already trying to scratch me!"

Perhaps the Stepmother is a woman caught in postpartum depression; she is bone dry, her emptiness so complete that mothering seems quite impossible. Too weary to feed herself, she might indeed feel that she's been "scooped out" by the infant at her breast. The withholding, wary Stepmother could be any parent so exhausted by the demanding helplessness of her family—husband *and* children—that she sees nothing but a lifetime of grueling care before her; she dreams of that lost paradise, of the time when she had no one to care for but herself. There are moments in the life of every mother when she has nothing left to give, when one more demand, it seems, would kill her. A child, in sensing this "famine in the land" will often push, demand more to quiet his anxiety. These are times of great inner need, the moments when Dark Mother and Devouring Child meet face to face. In the situation described below the scarcity felt at all levels seemed to constellate devouring greed in the children and an exacerbating, guilt-ridden withdrawal in the mother:

> Kate remembers the lean years following her divorce. She was in graduate school, living on a small grant: "My children were eight and ten, and they didn't get much of me. Between classes and practica and the odd jobs I took to buy groceries, I was gone twelve hours a day. When I got home they'd both be all over me, fighting for pieces of my body. They'd climb me like a mountain, and I'd want to scream them away, but I felt too guilty. It was terrible to watch them eat; they'd stuff themselves and fight over every grain of rice. I knew that they had enough to eat, and that that wasn't the problem at all. I'd sometimes bring a book to the table and try not to look at them."

Klein viewed the punishing, withholding mother as a construct of the child's inner life, a projection of his innate oral-sadism.[1] In theory, at least, she did not seem to allow for a child's accurately reading the rage of a depleted mother, nor for the mother's rejecting, self-protective responses to her demanding child. Her model, in short, did not adequately take in the vicissitudes of outer life.

Neumann, writing in post-Holocaust Israel, was surrounded by survivors of every sort of devastation; his perspective seemed to take in the chaos around him. He saw any disturbance—personal, cultural, environmental—in the "primal relationship", in the early, uroboric oneness of mother and child, as constellating both Dark Mother *and* Aggressive Child. Such disturbances, he theorized, would result in the child developing a "distress ego," an ego directed toward survival in an unwelcoming world:

---

[1] Fordham et al. (The Society for Analytical Society, London), in their efforts to integrate Kleinian and Jungian thought, have paid close attention to the role of the personal mother in mediating archetypal images for the child. Their ongoing work is largely based on close observation of mother-infant pairs, that is, on the interplay of human relationship and archetypal imagery. Cf. Sidoli, Mara, "De-integration and Re-Integration in the First Two Weeks of Life," *Journal of Analytical Psychology,* 1983, 28:201-212.

It is not true that "hate precedes love," or that the infant is in any primary sense cannibalistic and sadistic. Similarly, distrust in a child is not primary but is a reaction to distress.

When the ego becomes a distress-ego, whose experiences of the world, the Self and the thou is marked and characterized by hunger, insecurity and helplessness, The Good Mother becomes in like degree a negative and Terrible Mother. If the ego of this phase has already acquired a certain stability and independence, it becomes prematurely overaccentuated by way of compensation for this situation of distress and forsakenness....Where the primal relationship is disturbed, the distress ego is prematurely thrown back on itself; it is awakened too soon and *driven* to independence by the situation of anxiety, hunger and distress (Neumann, 1973, 77).

Hansel and Gretel have grown up in hard times. The family seems well acquainted with "anxiety, hunger and distress". As we meet the children in the story they are wary and vigilant; Hansel, at least, is in full possession of the street wisdom—the distress ego—of a child who has had to fend for himself:

> *Hunger had kept the children up as well, and they overheard their stepmother's plan. Gretel wept in fear, but Hansel comforted the girl and said, "God will protect us, sister dear, and I will find a way to help." With that, he crept outside and found white pebbles gleaming in the silver light of a full moon. He stuffed his pockets with the little stones, then went back into his room to sleep.*

Survivor that he is, Hansel has the ability—the hermetic consciousness—to perceive value in apparently ordinary objects. The pebbles carry the silver essence of the moon; they will be his guides. He stuffs his pockets with treasure, and returns to assure his sister that God will not forsake them. Like many children in desperate straits, he has a strong connection to archetypal parental images, images barely mediated by his personal parents: he looks to God the Father for protection, to the reflec-

tive Moon for guidance. These inner parents provide his sustenance.

I recall the first sandtray of a seven-year-old child referred by
his school for suicidal depression. His violent father was gone;
his well-meaning, but chronically depressed mother could offer
little support. His inner life, however, would prove rich and sus-
taining:

> The first object in the tray was a brown, big-breasted
> Buddha, arms joyfully uplifted. He placed it in the center of
> the tray, and followed with a church in the upper right-
> hand corner. To the left of the Buddha he placed an adult
> woman face down in the sand; she touched hands with an
> adult male, also lying face down. When he'd completed the
> tray with a school—sinking in the sand—and some animals
> grouped in front of the Buddha, he destroyed it all, over-
> turning all the objects with a small army tank. After a
> moment, having locked away the tank, he began to right
> the objects in the tray. He removed the adult figures, and
> placed a white, Wise-Old-Man figure next to the motherly
> looking Buddha. He'd judged his personal parents, and dis-
> posed of them; the Great Parents at the center would pro-
> vide whatever warmth and wisdom he would find.

Hansel and Gretel will need to marshal all their inner
resources; they are about to be sent into the cold, dark
world:

> *Before the sun was up next day, the woman roused the chil-*
> *dren from their beds. "Up, you lazy things! We must go to the*
> *forest and gather in some wood." With that, she gave each a*
> *piece of bread, and said, "There's your dinner now, and*
> *remember, that is all you'll get."*

One cannot fault the Stepmother for dishonesty here; she
offers nothing that she does not have; she creates no illusions.
This, she tells the children, is all there is. Ration it well. There is
something of the Stepmother's cruel honesty in setting the limits
of the analytic hour: we will meet at this time, in this place, and

only here. We will have just so many minutes; you will pay me for my time. In response to the patient's grinding hunger, to his awesome need, we offer one small (and, one hopes, nourishing) piece of bread. This much, no more.

Small children beginning treatment nearly always push the limits of the hour; there is always one more game they want to play, one more story to be told, another picture to be drawn. Ending time becomes the first great test of therapy, and of the therapist. Does she mean what she says? Can't she be moved to break the rules (and the vessel) just this once? Adults may be more subtle, but no less reluctant to accept the fifty-minute hour. I recall my second session with a young man who'd read psychology, but who'd never been in therapy before; he'd come, in part, for help with his cocaine abuse:

> At the end of the hour I announced that we were out of time. David seemed surprised and hurt. Shouldn't we spend some time summing things up, pulling things together? Perhaps we could do that, I told him, in the future, but we were out of time today. I assured him that he'd soon grow used to limits of the hour; his psyche would adjust. David nodded, started to get up, then sat down again, looking most distressed. He said, "I've thought of using coke this week." I suggested he make note of that for Monday, and I showed him to the door. My response felt brusque to me, and cold, but I could feel him tugging at me, pushing. I had to draw the line.

The Stepmother in our tale is more than clear about her limits, and Hansel hears her well. When his father chides him for his pokiness—he is dropping pebbles, one by one—he seems to know that his days of playful innocence have ended:

> *"I'm watching my white kitten on the roof; she wants to say good-bye."*

Like kittens set loose in the woods, Hansel and Gretel will be neither petted nor cared for; they must wave good-bye to childhood dependence. The Stepmother sees the dawning of this knowledge in the boy:

> *"Foolish boy, that is not your kitten on the roof, it is the rising sun."*

In the face of Stepmother limits, of hunger and imminent abandonment, Hansel is learning quickly, as he must. Neumann's "distress ego" follows on disaster, on hunger left unsatisfied too long. But even in the best of times, the child whose every need is immediately met develops not at all; he remains in Eden, in the uroboric paradise of Mother's arms. It is in frustration, in the tension of unanswered need, that ego grows.

John, the child whose initial sandtray is described above, was so needy at so many levels that it was important, and most painful, to hold to clear limits in his treatment. Who but a Stepmother could say no to this frail, hungry and engaging child? John never failed to note the Stepmother's presence in the room, never failed to call me by her name, but he did grow in his response to her. The session described below came in the third year of treatment; our weekly ritual of purchasing a snack at the corner store brought his hunger into sharp relief::

> John observed and understood my budgetary limits, and surprised me with his skill at making choices. At Eastertime, however, he set his sights on a chocolate rabbit costing twice the usual amount, and that was compromise; he really wanted a huge one at about twenty dollars. I held firm, and he pouted and stomped around the store, calling me several kinds of cheap. I waited, and he eventually suggested a solution: he'd skip his snack that day, and get the rabbit the next week. That is what we did. The next week, small rabbit in his hand, he grew morose, then angry. That huge rabbit taunted him. He raged on about the plushness of my office, about my large variety of toys, about all my unseen but fantasized possessions, none of which I'd share with him. Staring at the chocolate bunny, he said, "That little rabbit won't fill me up!" I agreed it would take many, many

rabbits to fill his empty places. He was quiet for a time, then had a revelation: "I know why you have all this stuff! You work all the time!" He began to fantasize about the work he'd do, the money he would make, the things he'd buy for himself and his family. In the hour he'd moved through his pain and envy to the possibility of nurturing himself.

For all their survivor's wisdom, even the most mistreated children retain a certain kind of dogged faith in their parents: "Someday," they believe, "they'll come through; if I am very good, my parents will surely be everything I need them to be, as perfect as every parent is. My mother will give me all I wish; my father will protect me from all danger." I don't think I've ever met a child in placement who did not yearn for home, who did not reinvent his parents in the yearning, cloak them in the mantle of archetypal good. The image of the perfect parent haunts and taunts us all.

In our story, the children *know* their parents' plan to leave them in the woods; Hansel has prepared for the worst. Still, the desire for good parenting can always overrule reality. The children allow themselves to be deceived, to mistake wind and withered tree for Father. They fall into their deep, unconscious need:

> When they'd reached the deepest woods, the father told the children to gather up some twigs, and he lit a fire to keep them warm. When the flames were high, their stepmother bade them rest themselves. "When we've done our work, we'll come back to fetch you home." Brother and sister rested by the fire and ate a bit of bread. They heard the strokes of a wood-axe and thought their father was near, for he'd fastened a branch to a withered tree, where the wind would blow it back and forth. Thus falsely comforted, they fell asleep.

When the children wake it is dark; they see they've been abandoned, left to starve in the great wood. They seem to feel no anger, only fear of this dark and unknown place. They dare not think too much about the welcome they'll receive at home, nor can they dwell upon the sort of parents who would leave them to their fate. Hansel leads his sister home on the moonlit, silver-pebble path he has prepared:

> *They walked all night, and when daylight dawned they saw their father's home*

Hansel and Gretel are greeted with less than wild enthusiasm by their father's wife:

> *Knocking at the door, they surprised their father's wife. "You wayward children, wherever have you been? We thought we'd not see you again!"*

I can imagine the Stepmother's distress: This was not her plan at all! Over the years it has often been my role to work with mothers whose children have been placed outside the home. At the outset, all libido moves toward the child's return; reunion is mother's most fervent hope. But as the time draws near the depleted Stepmother often finds her voice. Doubts set in, and the woman begins to act in ways guaranteed to turn the tide against return. Visitations go disastrously wrong; recovered alcoholics start to drink again; rent goes unpaid, food and shelter are suddenly at risk. At this point a most painful reassessment must take place: is it possible to conceive and bear a child one was never meant to raise? Might there be a home in which the Good Mother never had a chance, in which a state of inner poverty seems a permanent condition? There are women whose depth of unmet need is so great and terrible that it is all they can do to keep themselves alive, to mother the hungry wounded one within. When a woman consciously decides to let her child go—and this is true, I believe, in abortion as well—she must mourn her loss, and mourn the loss of the mother she had wished to be. There is wrenching guilt, the belief that to deny one's motherhood is some evil aberration, and there is also great relief. Freed of the Devouring Infant, the woman can begin to live, to heal herself. Her children are set free to invest their faith and loyalty in parents who can care for them.

The desire to return to the parental home surely goes beyond chronological childhood and material dependence. It is present in any search for "roots", in all nostalgia (from the Greek, *nostos:* a return, and *algos:* pain, grief), in every inner protest against "responsible adulthood." We return home with every dream of childhood place and face, with each association that brings us back to early memory. Home, however sweet or dark our memories of it may be, remains "the place where when you have to go there, they have to take you in" (Frost). James Hillman (1985) has some thoughts on the need for homecoming:

> Here we must remember that going home is always going *back* home. Returning is essentially a regressive act in keeping with the essential function of family: to provide shelter for the regressive needs of the soul. Everyone needs a place to crawl and lick his wounds, a place to hide and be twelve years old, inept and needy....Something always remains undeveloped and this piece needs to "go back home...."
>
> No one is at fault, no one is kicked out, and no one can be helped. Yet in this paralysis lies the profoundest source of acceptance...family love allows family pathology.

How does a depleted Stepmother respond to a child coming home with a bag full of dirty laundry and regressive needs? When reunions and holidays are over, is everyone expected to return to neutral corners, to scattered, independent living? Adult offspring returning to parental homes, often to lick the wounds of personal disaster, are now called "boomerang children"; parents refer to this new-old phenomenon as the "crowded nest syndrome." This language would not indicate a great and joyful welcome home; one hears the voice of the Stepmother: "What are you doing here? I thought I left you in the woods!"

I remember the great surge of relief I felt at my younger child's college graduation: "Done!" I thought, "My mothering is done. It is official. My children are both responsible adults!" At heart, I knew this sense of job-well-done to be illusory, knew that mother-child knots are not so easily untied, that no relationship so deep is ever quite complete. Still, for a day or so, I felt truly free, unbound! Today, I rejoice in and encourage homecomings. I spend hours singing in the kitchen, preparing everybody's favorite food, indulging in my own sort of nostalgia. But there are limits to my tolerance for ingathering. I soon begin to long for privacy, for quiet. The Stepmother enters then, bolts the door against intruders, and says, as clearly as she can: Enough!

The woodcutter's wife, looking at her empty larder, is again about to put the children out:

> *"All is gone," the woman said, "half a loaf of bread and that's the end of us. This time the children have to go, or we'll surely starve!"*

But one is never all that clear; it is never all that easy to close the door against familiar need. Behind the harsh and self-protective mother one can hear the voice of guilt and duty—the woodcutter, pleading for motherly self-sacrifice:

> *The woodsman hung his head and thought, "Better to share with them until we have no more." But she insisted, and let him have no peace.*

These dissonant parental voices, unresolved, may form the background music for a classic double bind. While the Good and Bad Parents argue at the door, a returning child may feel both welcomed and despised, pushed to leave and made to stay. A young woman presently living in her parents' home might prefer a simple "No!" to the ambivalence and guilt with which she lives:

Tiana and her two brothers, all in their mid-twenties, all caught in changes in careers and in relationships, live with their parents in what once seemed a comfortable and spacious home. Now there seems very little space, no privacy at all, none of the comforts one generally associates with home. No one feels free to entertain a guest, all are expected to keep to their own rooms; there are tensions around food, music, ringing phones. But when Tiana speaks of leaving, her parents seem hurt, and lecture her on practicalities; how, they ask, can she realistically afford to go?

Like this young woman and her brothers, Hansel and Gretel find themselves entrapped, forced into passivity.

Hearing this, Hansel tried to slip outside once more, but he found the door was locked.

The children can do nothing for themselves but wait. By morning, the Stepmother has quieted the voice of protest; she is ready to lead them to the woods, into the hands of nature. As the children are led off, Hansel pauses to make a breadcrumb trail, and to look back at his "pigeons, sitting on the roof." Until now Hansel and Gretel have instinctually sought home; like pigeons, they've set out only to return. Now, it would seem, that safety-seeking part of childhood must, too, be left behind. They'll be forced to take an unfamiliar path.

The woodsman's wife led them ever deeper in the wood, until they'd found a place they'd never been before.

They sleep, and waking in the dark, find themselves alone and without a road toward home. The birds, the guiding spirits of the forest, have moved them out of infancy by eating Hansel's breadcrumb trail. For the first time they are truly lost. The old path has disappeared and no new roads have opened up before them. At such moments in analysis it takes all the consciousness one has not to flee into denial and to remain in what a most courageous patient called "the gray place:"

Wendy came to analysis after having had a "flashback", a vague but terrifying memory of a childhood sexual assault. She was determined to learn "the truth," and her dreams had her engaged on searches through difficult terrain, down unfamiliar roads, through muddy bottomed jungles. As memory started to return and an image of father-as-assailant became clearer, Wendy felt lost, more frightened than she'd ever been before. If her father was a different man than

she'd imagined him to be for thirty years, what then was
true? Who and what could be relied upon? She found herself wanting desperately to *know,* to have it all spelled out
in black and white. At the same time, she wanted to deny
all knowledge, to close herself to memory. As it was, she
knew that she could only wait for what would come to her.
Waiting, remaining in the gray light of partial memory, was
most difficult of all.

The work, the waiting at such times may bring with it a wish
(shared by analyst and analysand) for numinous salvation, for a
dream, a glowing image, some guiding movement from within.
In the Humperdinck opera, Hansel and Gretel, in their evening
prayer, invoke the guidance of the guardian angels of the
night,

> *When at night I go to sleep,*
> *Fourteen angels watch do keep,*
> *Two my head are guarding, Two my feet are guiding,*
> *Two are on my right hand, Two are on my left hand,*
> *Two who warmly cover, Two to wake at dawn do hover*
> *Two to whom 'tis given, To guide my steps to Heaven!*
> *(Humperdinck and Wette, 1891)*

Hansel and Gretel wander for three days, deeper still into the
forest, until they hear the song of a beautiful white bird.
Salvation! They follow what must surely seem to them a holy
spirit as it leads them to an archetypal place of plenty, to a
house "built of bread and cakes...with windows of sugar."
Hansel and Gretel have found the essence of "Good Mother,"
and think themselves in heaven. In Bettelheim's (161) reading of
the tale,

> A gingerbread house, which one can "eat up," is a symbol
> of the mother, who in fact nurses the infant from her body.
> Thus the house at which Hansel and Gretel are eating away
> blissfully and without a care stands in the unconscious for
> the good mother, who offers her body as a source of nour-
> ishment. It is the original all giving mother, whom every
> child hopes to find again later somewhere out in the world,

when his own mother begins to make demands and to
impose restrictions."

The children respond to this unlimited, all-giving-mother-
house with an equally unlimited attack upon its bounty. They
have found themselves in a supra-human realm, and when questions come from within the house they respond as if they were
the spirit of divinity:

> ...*a small voice came from within,*
>
> *"Do I hear a little mouse?*
> *Who is nibbling on my house?"*

The children answer:

> *"Tis only the wind,*
> *The heavenly wind,"*

and go right on with their nibbling. They are, at this moment,
Divine Children of the Perfect Mother, well beyond ordinary
human limitation. They've taken on the devouring greed of the
Kleinian Child:

> *Hansel, who liked the tasty roof, tore down great chunks to*
> *feed himself...Gretel pushed out a candy window pane...*

And, as such a child might imagine (in projection and in reality as well), they raise the wrath of the archetypal Witch:

> *There suddenly appeared a woman older than the hills.*

In working with abused, neglected children, with the Hansels
and Gretels of any age, the therapist feels a great pull to be the
Good-and-Understanding, All-Giving-Mother, to compensate
such patients for their loss. When patients respond, as do the
children in this tale, with primitive, ungovernable greed, one is
suddenly confronted with much more than can be handled in
the hour. This child could eat the therapist alive! At this moment

the Stepmother intrudes herself into the playroom in all her self-protective rage, sweeping aside all therapeutic notions of one-sided saintliness and generosity.

One of my students recently described her first encounter with this Dark Mother of the playroom: she'd brought a cake and some small gifts to celebrate her patient's sixth birthday, but she was quite unprepared for the deeply regressive, birth-day acts which followed. The child curled up in a corner and cried for a bottle, then needed to be held. The therapist spent most of the hour rocking and singing to a six-year-old suddenly turned infant:

> After some time I let her know it was time to get ready to return to school. She jumped out of my lap and grabbed one of the teddy bears I keep on hand, insisting that it was one of her birthday gifts. I reasoned with her, reminded her of rules about the office toys, but she would not let it go. She told me I was mean and ugly and boring; the bear would be much happier going home with her. I felt myself growing angry and possessive; that was *my* bear, and I didn't want it going to her dirty, awful house. I talked to her more forcefully, and I finally pried the bear out of her grip. She screwed up her face and screamed like an angry infant. I was horrified with myself, I could see the hurt and disappointment in her eyes, but I wasn't sorry that I'd taken back the bear. It was mine!

The therapist, in meeting this dark and angry one within herself, gained an understanding of this child and her family she'd never had before. The abuse the child still suffered in her home no longer seemed an aberration when viewed in context of relationship; the child had some part in the exchange, however small. That part would yield itself to consciousness, to deep interpretation, and the child could begin to change. Despite the therapist's initial fears, the incident made for a greater bond between the two; they'd shared one another's darkness.

The old woman in this tale keeps the mean, devouring aspect of herself well hidden, and stays with her sweet persona at least long enough to lure the hungry children in:

> *In the house, she fed them cakes and fruit and milk, then led*
> *them to two feather beds laid with clean white linen cloth.*
> *Hansel and Gretel rested well, and felt they were in heaven*
> *after all.*

We are then informed as to her true intent:

> ...the old one was far from kind. In truth, she was an evil,
> child-eating witch, and she'd made the candy house to draw
> the chidlren in. When a child came close enough she'd kill
> it, cook it, and set her table for a feast.

We should not be surprised to find this devouring one within
the witch's sticky-sweet exterior. Just as the cold, rejecting
Stepmother forced the children out into the world, well into ego-
growth, the Witch, in inviting them inside for milk and cookies,
may well imprison them, eat them, keep them within herself forever. Neumann (1963:38) speaks of this interplay of "Good" and
"Terrible" in Mother with concomitant regression and transformation in the child:

> Thus a goddess can be a Good Mother in whom the ele-
> mentary character is predominant, or she may reveal traits
> of the Terrible Mother with a predominance of the transfor-
> mative character. Both characteristics are significant for the
> situation of the ego and consciousness. The Good Mother
> can, for example, be associated with an infantile ego and
> then be typical for a negative development situation. An
> example is the witch in the fairy tale of Hansel and Gretel,
> whose house, i.e. exterior, is made of gingerbread and
> candy, but who in reality eats little children. Conversely, the
> Terrible mother may be associated with a tendency toward
> the transformative character...her appearance may introduce
> a positive development in which the ego is driven toward
> masculinization and the fight with the dragon, i.e. positive
> development and transformation.

The Witch, "a woman older than the hills," has always lain in
wait for poor and hungry children weary of their journey
through the woods. She seems to exist in response to the harsh

Stepmothers of reality, those who send their children out to struggle in the world. She is the Mother to whom libido flows in terrified regression when psyche cannot deal with here and now. The lost children are familiar figures in the darkness of her forest:

> *When Hansel and Gretel approached she laughed with glee,*
> *and thought: "These little ones shall not escape again!"*

Whenever we are drawn, in the presence of a hungry patient, to be very sweet, we are open to the most dangerous of therapeutic traps; the Witch awaits within. In our efforts to be good, to be nurturing and kind (perhaps, to give the patient what we most want for ourselves), we can infantilize the object of our goodness right out of consciousness. A patient recently complained to me about her previous experience with a warm, supportive therapist. I could hear the warning in her words:

> She fed me balderdash support! When I felt oppressed she
> sympathized, and condemned the people who had hurt me.
> How could they do that to wonderful me? There was no
> chance to look at my own part in things. I knew that I was
> far from wonderful—that's why I'd come for therapy!—but
> she wouldn't see my evil, or let me see it for myself.

The same patient, in the beginning of our work, had talked about her ending with this therapist:

> It was so strange; I think she was a very gentle person, but
> I began to see her as a witch, with long red fingernails
> ready to come at me and tear me up.

The Witch in our tale locks young Hansel in a cage, there to be fattened for the kill. As Uroboric Mother, the all-enclosing one, she has effectively cut off the boy's heroic forward thrust; he will be hers forever. This sweetly devouring one lies so deep in the collective psyche that we see her everywhere. She is lovely, jealous Aphrodite punishing her darling Eros for his dalliance with Psyche (Graves, 1951); She is Portnoy's Sophie, drowning him in chicken soup (Roth, 1969); She is the public welfare system with its iron/velvet grip on those for whom it cares too well, and She is certainly the mourning mother who said of her dead son: "Well, I'd rather have him like that than give him away to another woman" (Von Franz, 1981).

In seeing Her everywhere, however, we may not be seeing her at all. She is such an easy, ever-present target that we can attack her blindly, without reflection, and still be sure of striking a responsive chord. We might say of Hansel that "he is caught in the Mother," and feel that we have said it all, have defined the problem and its solution in the simplest of terms. Hansel must kill the Witch, must slay this awful Dragon, and get on with his heroic life.

What we may fail to see is Hansel's collusion in the process of imprisonment. He has been caught by the Devouring One while attempting to devour her. He's been entrapped by his great and overwhelming hunger, but once caught, he exaggerates his neediness and makes the most of his imprisonment. When he holds out a bone in lieu of a finger, he is using a stratagem to prolong his life. At another level, he is prolonging his very special treatment at the Witch's hands.

Now Hansel had the richest food...

If he's to be a prisoner, he will enjoy it. A delightful modern version of the tale has him asking, from the confines of his cage, for "more cakes and cream, and perhaps a goose now and then" (Maly, 1987). If Hansel is not quite a victim here, is the Witch wholly a villainess? Who is devouring whom?

> Tess and her fiancé planned to marry in the spring, but there remained the problem of his widowed mother. The young man had always lived with her, but her health was poor, her disposition sour, and she was more demanding with every passing year. Tess could not imagine living in the widow's home, but her fiancé, as much as he complained about his mother's hold on him, could not imagine leaving her. He lived rent free, his clothes were washed, his meals prepared. Someday, he told his bride-to-be, his

mother would be gone and then he'd own the house. The old woman held him very close, but not without his full cooperation.[2]

While Hansel suffers his imprisoned luxury, Gretel is now treated like the proverbial Stepchild:

> ...*Hansel had the richest food, while Gretel had naught but crab-shells and hard work.*

I am reminded of another tale, "The Girl and the Dead Man" (Hyde, 1979), in which a mother offers each of her departing daughters a choice: they may have a small piece of bread for the journey, and her blessing, or a large piece and her curse. The older girls choose the large piece and meet unhappy ends. The youngest takes the small piece, and her mother's blessing. With this, she makes her way in the world. So it seems with Gretel. Beyond the initial sweet seductions, she is offered nothing in the Witch's house but the demands of grueling work, and the opportunity to face the Witch and learn from her. This may seem a questionable blessing, but it is just what Gretel needs to come into her own, to feel her strength.

Until now she has been quite passive and dependent on her brother's care. Hansel, taking a leaf from his Stepmother's book, has seen to their survival, while she, much like their father, has wept and worried and wrung her hands. As the Witch advises her, this will no longer do at all:

> *Stop that noise, your tears won't help a bit!*

On her own now, Gretel keeps her eyes open, watches the Witch most carefully, and senses the trap laid out for her.

> *"First we'll bake," said the old witch, "come see if the oven's hot and ready for the dough." But Gretel suspected*

---

[2] Sadly, the young man's inheritance was of a different sort. He died of acute alcoholism at the age of twenty-six.

that the witch would eat her too, and pretended not to know what was afoot.

Gretel has learned her lessons well. She is able to use the Witch's ruse against her; she tricks the trickster and lures her to her death. The Witch puts her own head in the oven, and Gretel,

> *...pushed the old one from behind, and bolted fast the iron oven door. The witch howled and screamed for mercy as she burnt to death.*

Even the half-blind Witch can see that her end has come. Gretel has outsmarted her, pushed her into her own cake-and-cookie death-trap. How does overworked, newly independent, observant Gretel work in psyche? What is the push that kills the Sweet Devouring One, leaving her "burnt out," unable and unwilling to kill with kindness as she's always done? Often a change of consciousness, brought on by a major life crisis, is enough to bring one's self-entrapment into unavoidably clear focus.

> Barbara spent the twenty-five years of her marriage tending to her children's and her husband's every need. She also managed the family with an iron hand. Ten years ago her widowed, alcoholic father joined the household and the ranks of those in Barbara's control. Barbara worked very hard, but she was unequivocally in charge.
>
> With the ending of her marriage Barbara suddenly saw things in a very different light. She wanted to get away, start over, but her father needed care, her children, although young adults, still wanted her at home, and her husband seemed unable to realize that he'd have to manage on his own. She was caught in a trap of her own making, and realized it, but it would take a tremendous act of will to kill the inner Witch, to let her familiar power go, and to consciously, selectively, start saying, "No!"

When the wicked, sweet-devouring Witch is killed, burnt out, she creates a void in psyche which may well be filled by the cold, rejecting Stepmother, the woodcutter's self-protective wife. The mother who has always been too willing to provide will find herself so totally depleted that she'll turn her back on her dependents, shut down, and turn everyone away. What we may see then is deep, intractable depression, perhaps a suicide. A great dearth will have fallen on the land, and our story might well begin again. But "Hansel and Gretel" has a happier conclusion: *both* Dark Mothers die, and the children, set free, return to a home where "worries came no more." Their activities between the Witch's death and their arrival at their father's door may well make all the difference.

> *...as they now had no more to fear, they went back into the witch's house. They found it piled high with treasures of all kinds...*

When we can move past our fear of being eaten up alive, we may well find treasure in the Witch's house. So much of analysis is involved in imaginal revisits to a childhood home, in discovering and naming the witches and demons that we find there. It seems to me that that is only half the work. The safe container of analysis (in a sense, The Good Mother) provides the ground for encountering the Witch; she is right there in the transference, constellated by the patient's need. In analysis, to the degree that She is consciously carried by the analyst, She may be faced and fought without retaliation. When the long-imprisoned, rageful child-within is freed, when he or she has "killed" the dreadful child-eating witch of memory, the work to find a place in family, to find family's place within ourselves, begins. If, in returning to the sweet and bitter prisons of our childhood, we look carefully enough, we may find unexpected riches where there once seemed only traps and cages and frightful dragons to be slain.

Portnoy's Complaint, Philip Roth's roast of the Devouring Mother, ends with the words:

"So [said the doctor], Now vee may perhaps to begin. Yes?"

And Roth, twenty years beyond *Portnoy's Complaint,* and several years after his mother's death, says of her,

My mother was really no problem. As soon as my brother
and I started giving genuine signs of burgeoning independence, she had relaxed the exacting...strictures that had
governed our early upbringing....[My brother] seems as a
child to have felt more constrained by her vigilant mothering than I ever did, though he, no less than I, found more
than a little sustenance in the inexhaustible maternal feeling
that visibly instigated and tenderized that conscientious-
ness."[3]

A patient, after years of battling with her mother, said of her
recently:

Three years ago her doctors thought she had a month or
two to live, her heart was weak, her kidneys were almost
gone; anything could finish her. But she was determined to
go on, and to everyone's surprise, she just grew stronger. I
see now that she has incredible tenacity, strength I never
gave her credit for. I have some of that doggedness myself,
and I wonder how much more she's left me that I thought
was mine and mine alone. I hope I can find a way to tell
her how much I admire her.

This acknowledgement of treasure in the Witch's house is the
gratitude that is the counterforce to envy in Klein's model of
development, the experience which can transform the
Devouring Infant into a person capable of love:

...the weakening of projections, and therefore the achieving
of greater tolerance, bound up with less resentment, make it
possible for the patient to find some features and to revive
pleasant memories of the past, even when the early situation was very unfavorable....All this becomes possible
because the integration resulting from the analysis has
strengthened the ego, which was weak at the beginning of
life....object synthesis, and therefore a mitigation of hate by
love, come about, and greed and envy...lose in
power....Capacity for enjoyment and gratitude increases
step by step." (234)

---

[3]Again, in his 1991 memoir, *Patrimony,* Roth lovingly takes in his irascible father, understanding that his "patrimony" is his father's wholeness, good and bad.

Hansel and Gretel, having filled their pockets with the Witch's bounty, are ready to begin the journey home. They'll return with a degree of self-sufficiency not likely to raise the presence of their father's wife. Indeed, when they return, they find her gone; she is no longer constellated by their neediness. The children now need only leave the forest. There is nothing to be feared at home.

Leaving the forest, however, is no simple task. The children are confronted with "a great stretch of water" where there had been no such obstacle before. Hans Dieckmann (39) says of this change in the scenery:

> Where previously a transitionless intermingling of the two worlds obtained and the normal world of the woodcutter simply turned into a magical region, now a great, broad body of water separates the two realms....We find a lack of delineation between consciousness and the unconscious primarily in a still immature and labile ego....In the case of the stable and healthy ego, on the other hand, there exists a clear boundary between the two realms.

The children have survived abandonment and near starvation, they've defeated the devouring Witch, they've found the treasure hidden in the Witch's house. All of this has brought them to the great water, to a moment of decision. Do they cross that boundary into consciousness, and leave behind the realm of magic, of gingerbread and dreadful witches? I've seen children—and adults—struggle with this moment, pause at the river's edge and wet their feet before plunging in to personal responsibility. Zach, at six years old, seemed to make an irrevocable decision.

> Zach spent a year attributing his poor behavior to a monster living in his closet. This monster might do awful things, but Zach himself, he told me, would never pee in his brother's toy chest, never curse his mother when she punished him, never cheat at games. We spoke of this monster often, while Zach. maintained his halo. There were some changes, some taming of the monster, and Zach spent the summer with his grandparents. When he returned, as a serious first-

grader carrying his books, I alluded to the ghosts we'd imagined inhabiting my office the year before. He shook his head sadly and told me, "Jackie, there are no ghosts, and no monsters either!" His attitude had changed remarkably; in a few weeks our work was done.

Hansel cannot see a way to cross the river, and it seems to be his turn to wring his hands while his sister seeks help in the spiritual environment. Grace does appear in the form of yet another winged creature, a courier as much at home in water as in the air, but Gretel is too wise to put too much weight on their continuing good luck. Their journey will require patience, trust, and a degree of autonomy from one another:

> *The duck came by, Hansel sat himself upon its back and called his sister to sit down as well. But Gretel waited, saying, "Together we're too heavy for this little duck. You go, then send her back for me." Thus they crossed, one after the other...*

The greedy children who wanted everything at once no longer travel with them. Nor is Gretel so attached to Hansel that she fears his going on ahead. Brother and sister are close and loving, but they are separate beings now. Each brings home a pocketful of jewels, that is, a clearer sense of self.

Conclusion

> *Thus ends my tale, and a mouse runs across the room. Catch it, and make yourself a fine fur cap.*

This last line of the tale sums up its philosophy: that which most frightens us brings us our greatest opportunities. Hansel and Gretel are survivors, children with the hermetic capacity to catch a fur cap as a mouse runs across the room. They exemplify the miraculous resiliency of psyche, the capacity to transcend early deprivation and abandonment and still find precious jewels contained within the pain.

But my interest here is with the women, with the Stepmothers in this tale. They reject and imprison, starve and over-gratify, spit out and devour. Together, they surround Mother with her shadow; at the moment that she turns away from one she is in danger of falling in the other. At best, she can hope to walk a narrow, conscious line between the two. While it is a truism of family work that over-protective, too indulgent mothers mask their true rejection of the child, the opposite, I believe, is also true. The rejecting mother fears her inner Witch, the one who would deplete her, use her up, in an effort to hold her child in a tight embrace. In response to the demanding child we fall toward one Dark Mother or the other, trying to maintain some balance as we move between the two. The danger is in over-compensation, in the wish to say, "No, I am not like that at all!" When we escape the woodcutter's wife we are in the Witch's forest. When we've burnt out in the Witch's hearth the Stepmother may well wait for us at home.

Still, for all the dangers they present, these doubly Dark Mothers are psychological necessities. Children do more than survive their indulgence and rejection; *they grow through them.* The woodcutter's wife surely fosters independence, the move toward personal autonomy. The Witch's House is shelter for those moments when deep regression, a return to the matrix of our being, is the necessary path of healing. As long as there are Needy Children, there will be Stepmothers there to push and pull, to take us in and put us out.

The story has both Dark Mothers die, and this seems directly related to the growing independence of the children. When Needy Infants learn to feed themselves, so says this tale, they are freed of the Withholding Mother *and* the Devouring Witch. As individuals with the capacity for self-nurturance they are no longer at the mercy of primitive, overpowering need. They neither constellate the self-protection of the breast-denying Stepmother, nor are they likely to be drawn to the sweet entrapment of the Witch. Mothers and children create and recreate each other all the time; neither exists in the absence of the other.

This story offers one last parting jewel. As a therapist working individually with children, I've sometimes been asked to justify my work. What is the point in treating a child when he is, in fact, a powerless victim of family pathology? Shouldn't therapy be focused on the family system, or toward the parents as perpetrators of abuse? "Hansel and Gretel" seems responsive to these vital ethical and therapeutic questions: the children portrayed in this tale may indeed be victims, but they are hardly powerless in their capacity to effect change within the family. Like many children of abuse, they are the family members most amenable to change and growth, most open to guidance from the Self. When Hansel and Gretel meet the challenges set before them they return home laden with the treasures of their journey. They carry change within themselves, and through them, family healing can begin.

4

"CINDERELLA" AND THE LOSS OF FATHER-LOVE

In my work with young children I have always been moved by the child's miraculous ability to find and use just those materials—games, stories, images, even pieces of furniture—best suited for the healing of his or her wounds. So it was with Ginny, the quick and independent sister of a chronically ill child. Given her sister's special needs, Ginny was always second in her parents' hearts and minds; her frequent misbehavior was her only means of briefly holding center stage. In therapy she learned to use her hours in most expressive ways, directing me to play the role of rescuer/protector/friend, Godmother, Good Fairy or the Prince. At not quite four years of age, "Cinderella" was her chosen tale.

> Ginny's favorite made-up game was to run into the waiting room and hide in a space behind her mother's chair. In my part as Prince, I was to enter with an object, meant to be a shoe, in hand. I'd make a show of searching for the proper foot to fit the shoe, then discover Ginny in her niche. Thus found, she'd emerge in triumph from behind the chair, try on the "shoe", and prance around the room, a tiny Cinderella ready to be seen and loved.

"Cinderella" is a story for the Stepchild in us all, for the lonely one waiting for her Prince, for the one who feels unseen by those she loves. We weep with Cinderella when we feel harried and abused, when a Stepmother within warns against our dreams. Joy, she seems to say, is gold that will surely turn to lead at the stroke of twelve. Cinderella's triumph at the ball is a victory for all who'd prove Stepmother wrong, who would naysay her mocking, deprecating voice. When Cinderella dances with The Prince she dances for all who dare to wish for love, for recognition, for better days to come.[1]

When we recall the Cinderellas of our youth we probably remember Disney's lovely, laughing film, or the genteel stories of Perrault, in which a graciously forgiving Cinderella brings her sisters to her royal court.[2] The Grimms' Germanic version that we'll look at here is a darker tale, bloody and vengeful and full of mutilating loss.[3] Like most Stepmother tales, this "Cinderella" is a tale of grief. It begins, fittingly, with Mother's death-bed scene:

> *The wife of a wealthy man fell ill, and was close to death. As her end drew near, she called her beloved daughter to her side, and said: "My dear and only child, remember to be pious and be good. God, then, will protect you, and I shall watch from heaven and be ever near." With that she died. The young girl visited her mother's grave each day and wept,...*

In this bereavement tale, every member of the family responds to loss. Cinderella weeps and pines in her attachment

---

[1] A recent version of this tale, the movie *Pretty Woman*, takes great pleasure in proving the disapproving wrong. The heroine, dressed in her newly purchased clothes, returns to the store where she'd been insulted and ignored the day before. The look of shocked recognition on the saleswomen's faces sends a cheer up in the audience every time the film is shown.

[2] C.F. Neil Philip, *The Cinderella Story: The Origins and Variations of the Story Known as "Cinderella,"* for the history and evolution of this tale. In 1892, M.R. Cox compiled 345 variants of "Cinderella" in a collection reissued by Kraus Reprinted Limited in 1967.

[3] Children take great pleasure in the gory details of this tale, in which they find their fantasies of vengeance played out to the full. Adults, on the other hand, are shocked and prefer the prettied versions they recall.

to her grief; Stepmother and her daughters carry coldness and envy in their hearts, while father meets their cruel, unconscious power with an equally unconscious weakness and withdrawal. Cinderella is not the only orphan in this tale; her stepsisters have suffered loss and will suffer more throughout this tale, as cruelty turns upon itself in a mockery of Mother Love. The story begins with the Good Mother's death, ends with her punishing revenge and is taken up throughout with a desperate search for masculine security and love. When Mother dies, Father's love is lost as well, buried in the coldness of his grief.

> *Winter came and went, and with the Spring the man had found another wife. The woman had two daughters of her own, beautiful like she, but vile in temperament and black of heart.*

Cinderella's father takes a wife to ease his family's pain. Instead, he brings home grief equal to his own; each family amplifies the others' need. This "proud and haughty" Stepmother[4] has no softness for her husband's child; her widowhood has left her hard and dry. Her husband and the father of her family has gone, and she's raised two daughters as lonely and unhappy as herself. "Beautiful and fair of face" they may well be, but they seem to lack a lens through which to view the beauty that is theirs. It brings them little joy.

The bereavement that binds all the women in this tale— Stepmother, her daughters, surely the heroine herself—is that of father-loss. Each plays out an aspect of this loss, Cinderella in her flights from love, her sisters in their wish to win the Prince, Stepmother in her desperate need to see her daughters wed. She has had to raise her family alone, and her pride and haughtiness may well be her defense against the helplessness she has felt along the way. She's determined that her daughters have a better life than she, a life safely in a husband's care. Her

---

[4]So she is described in Perrault's French version of the tale, in which Stepmother is also called "the most disagreeable lady in the whole country." (Philip, 1989), and (Howell, 1985).

stepchild is a mere distraction from her overall campaign, another burden in her overburdened life.

Fathers have played minor, seemingly unimportant, roles in the other tales we've looked at here. In "The Laidly Worm...," and in "Snow White," the widowed fathers seek and find their second wives, and then all but disappear, seemingly enchanted by the witches in their homes. "Hansel and Gretel"'s Woodsman-Father can do little more throughout the tale than wring his hands. In each of these tales, a son or brother or some passing foreign prince has appeared to defeat the Witch, rescue the princess and bring balance and completion to the tale. These young heroes are stepping into Father's shoes, for once-upon-a-time the Old King was a hero too, with a vitally important role in family life.

Neumann (1973:198) sees Father as the bearer of "tradition, culture and the development of consciousness," without whom the child might be lost in a maternal uroboric state. In familial terms, one might understand Father as a necessary third to the perfect twoness of the mother-child bond. His presence moves the child from the paradise of mother's arms into an awareness of others in the world, and thus into awareness of himself as separate being. This archetypal Father carries conflict, therefore consciousness, into the child's life.

In Freudian terms, the Oedipal father stands between a mother and her son, challenging the child to take him on or to forego instinctual desire. A daughter, too, must give up her desire for her father, but not before experiencing, at a feeling level, the mutuality of that desire. Father's love, returned, is an acknowledgement of her as a sexual being. Samuels (1986) speaks to the importance of this relationship in feminine development:

> [The] erotic element guarantees the significance of the relationship....The father could not be more different from his daughter; he is male and from another generation. This is what gives him his potential to stimulate an expansion and deepening of her personality. But he is also part of the same family as his daughter; that should make him "safe" as regards physical expression of this necessary sexuality and also provides a reason for his own emotional investment.

Aside from his role in his childrens' development, father's greatest contribution to a family's life may be in his support of mother in her nurturing and containing role. Ideally, he provides her with a place of rest, with a means of regathering her strength and her stores of loving care. A year ago I joined family and friends in the huge public picnic that marks Boston's celebration of the Fourth of July. A young woman sat among us and nursed her infant child, while her husband knelt beside her, feeding her while she fed their son. The small circle they created for themselves was so protective and complete that neither the surrounding crowd nor the fireworks could disturb their peace. In the absence of Father, this loving and protective third to the mother-child pair, the demands of mothering may make Stepmothers of us all. A depleted, isolated mother has less and less to give her child, and raising one's family alone may well evoke the Witch:

> Janet's husband, a submariner in the nuclear fleet, spent half his year at sea, three months on shore, three months on the sub. The first month of his sea-time went relatively well; Janet, warmed by the last weeks of his time with her, felt cared-for and relaxed, and while she missed him she could feel his presence in their home. Her children felt this too, and joined her in her efforts toward a structured family life. By the second month they'd begin to test her limits and her will, and her unsupported weariness would begin to show: the grass would go unmowed, dishes go unwashed, and she'd lose her patience earlier each day. By the time the petty officer returned he'd find his children wild, his home a mess and his wife a screaming hag. They'd repair the damage over several weeks, but by then it was nearly time for him to leave again.

Father's absence need not be so stark to bring Stepmother to the scene. His partial withdrawal, born of helplessness and fear, and played out in rigidity of roles, can be just as keenly felt and not so easily addressed:

> Anne was five, her brother seven, when her parents were divorced. Her father, at a loss for how to spend his week-

end visit time with her, left her with his new young bride
while he and brother washed the car, mowed the lawn and
made household repairs. The four would meet only around
meals. No one openly complained; father, after all, was a
conscientious man trying hard to do his best. As one might
guess, his wife and daughter blamed one another for their
loneliness and loss, and their shared resentment grew into
week-end dread. The stepmother acted out her archetypal
role and Anne responded as a weepy, angry stepchild in
her father's home.

"Cinderella" brings the theme of father-loss into sharp relief.
In no other tale is his distance quite so darkly felt, his grief-
borne blindness to the women's needs so stark. He takes no
protective role in any version of the tale, and in some he is altogether gone. A Spanish "Cinderella"[5] has it thus:

> All were very happy for some months, until the father had
> to take a long trip, from which he never returned. With the
> absence of [Cinderella's] father, things began to change...

We can imagine the rage and disappointment in Cinderella's
home. A widow remarries, seeking that second chance at life:
comfort, warmth, an end to loneliness; a partner in parenting
her difficult, demanding girls. Instead, she finds herself in sole
charge of a grieving child, a child so attached to mourning that
ashes seem her natural milieu. The widow, having been
betrayed into a caretaker's role, is clearly having none of it; she
has no comfort left to give. The child becomes the target of her
wrath and her daughters join her in her outraged sense of loss.
They've made do with very little loving parent-care, and scarcity
has fed their greed. They are not about to share the little that
they have.

> *...the sisters plagued her with their insults and their ugly
> ways. They took her pretty clothes and bade her dress in*

---

[5]Tardy, William T., Treasury of Children's Classics in Spanish and English, Lincolnwood,
National Textbook Company, 1987.

rags and wooden shoes. "Where is the proud princess
now?" they laughed, and had her work from dawn to
dusk...

What deprivation lies behind the sisters' mocking cries, their
need to taunt the grieving girl? Do they sense in her her mother's parting gift, the ever present nearness of the love they have
never known? Like Psyche's sisters, they must destroy this
stranger Eros in their midst, that which never has been, never
can be, theirs. Love, beginning with a love of self, is an alien
invader in their home, always longed for, always pushed away.

How does one empathize with ugliness, with the heartless
lack of empathy played out by the sisters in this tale? Sitting with
such darkness in an analytic hour is the most difficult of therapeutic tasks, for it constellates one's hateful sister when an
understanding soulmate is the patient's desperate need:

> Beth, the fourth of seven girls, spent her childhood vying
> for her mother's ear, her father's eye. She feels today that
> she was never truly seen or heard. At thirty-five she is tal-
> ented, quite beautiful, and by her own sad doing, utterly
> alone. At family gatherings she provokes her sisters and
> their mates until they turn their backs on her and leave.
> She undermines her colleagues, challenges her boss and
> throws away her lovers whenever they want loving in
> return. I am often flooded with revulsion as she tells her
> tales; she seems so totally devoid of the capacity for empa-
> thy and love. Finally, at the nadir of my own disgust, I find
> that I am with her after all. The rage, and the separateness
> from her I feel are what she suffers through every hour of
> her life. I have a glimpse into the depth of her misery and
> pain.

The suffering of the "vile and black of heart" can be profound—a hopeless, lonely journey that would seem to have no
end. In a gathering following one of my "Stepmother" talks, a
young woman handed me this poem, then slipped away:

THE UGLY STEPSISTER

I am an ugly stepsister.
Never have I lovingly done work.
Only cried and wanted to be rescued
By the Prince divinely dancing.
But my feet
They're too big.
Size nine.
Some seem to think
I could have been
    Cinderella if I'd only tried.
She who was born from love
And knew her true worth.
What did I have to sing about?
          —D.M., Vancouver

What to sing about, indeed? A young woman growing up needs a mother, well-grounded in her own femininity, with whom she can identify if she's to value the woman in herself. Cinderella's mother, close to her child even in the moment of her death, provides the girl with that sense of self that shines through all her ashes and her tattered clothes. This centeredness provokes the envy that her sisters feel. The sisters, it would seem, lack that model in their lives; they've only known their mother in her darkness, in the incompleteness of her widow's grief. Worse, they've missed the sparkle in their father's eye, the admiring glance that can take a daughter's beauty in and return it to her with delight and love. Without that loving and reflective eye, what can these sisters know of their true worth? Samuels continues:

> Many fathers and daughters fail to achieve this [erotic] link. This is because men tend to be extremely cautious about becoming erotically involved with their daughters (even in fantasy)....The father's failure to participate in a mutual attraction and mutual, painful renunciation of erotic fulfillment with his daughter deprives her of psychological enhancement. This can take many forms: mockery of her sexuality, over-strictness, indifference—and, if the symbolic

dimension is savagely repressed, actual incest. In the absence of eros or its excess the daughter loses sight of herself as a sexually viable adult, with disastrous consequences. (Samuels, 1986)

All that the sisters in this tale know about father is his absence in their lives. Their loss is so profoundly felt it can only be expressed in surface greed, in a need for all the glitter that the world provides:

One day, when [Cinderella's] father was about to travel to the nearest town, he asked his step-daughters what he might bring them from the fair. "Pretty dresses," said the one, while her sister asked for emeralds and pearls.

Their wish, in its essence, is to be remembered while father journeys to and from the fair. The child (of any age) who assaults the returning traveler with cries of "What did you bring for me?" wants to know that he was missed along the way. Cinderella has what seems, at first, to be a different sort of wish, but she, too, needs to be carried in her father's mind; good mothering is never quite enough:

"Father, bring me the first branch to touch your hat as you ride toward home."

Nature herself seems to tap father on the head. He returns with a hazel twig, a symbol of hidden wisdom, divine inspiration and the Earth Goddess's chthonic powers (Cooper, 80). A grateful Cinderella plants the twig on her mother's grave:

The Hazel twig, watered by Cinderella's many tears, grew to be a handsome tree, and a small white bird nestled in the tree and granted Cinderella's every wish.

This bird—the departed mother's spirit, always near—brings Cinderella everything but her father's loving eye. He seems to be oblivious to the abuse she suffers at her sisters' hands, nor does he see the envy eating at his stepdaughters' hearts. Could this father be determined not to see the younger women in his home, in an effort to deny the erotic energy he feels? In "Thousandfurs" (Grimm, #65), a variant on the Cinderella theme, a King is enjoined to incest by his dying wife; he promises to marry no one not as beautiful as she. As his daughter grows to be the beauty that her mother was, she becomes the object of the King's desire, and must protect herself by running off, hidden in a cloak of many furs. In family life, fathers may protect their daughters and themselves from their desires by turning a blind eye, by not seeing the young beauties growing up before their eyes. While father-daughter incest, acted out, may be the worst sort of sexual abuse, this denial of incestuous desire abuses sexuality in its most delicate and nascent state (cf. Samuels, above). When father turns away in fear, the admiring glances of a passing Prince may take on great importance for a Princess coming into bloom:

> Kate remembers the party for her "Sweet Sixteen", one of her first dates with the boy she'd eloped with at eighteen: "I'd had my hair cut short that day in a becoming style and I wore a dance dress I'd picked out for myself. When my father saw me he was furious, and told me I looked ugly, like some sort of tramp. Even I could see that wasn't so, but he had me close to tears. J. arrived just then and he was so impressed he could barely speak; I was a different girl than the one he'd seen that afternoon in school! The look on his face meant everything to me."

The longed for Prince may arrive in more pernicious forms. In Chapter One we looked at brother-sister incest as a saving grace. When kept at the level of desire, this intensity of sibling love serves as container for familial eros, for love that has no other place to go. Sadly, separating action from desire is at times too great a task for a child prince to bear. Brother-sister incest, acted out and then repressed, becomes a hidden source of shame in adult life, a shadow on one's erotic life.

> Gwen and her brother Josh grew up with a father who'd learned to keep his feelings under wraps. He viewed his

wife and children from an icy distance that left all in a state of aching need. At some time early in their lives Gwen and Josh discovered comfort in one another's sexual touch. Gwen cannot yet say when this activity began, nor when it ceased to be. She only knows that pleasure, now, is inextricably bound with shame; her body's needs evoke her greatest fears.

In our tale, as in the memory above, father's distance keeps everyone in a state of need. As we might expect, the announcement of the Prince's Ball stirs a flurry of excitement in Cinderella's home:

> *The king in those days had a son, and the son was looking for a bride. Accordingly, the King ordered that a feast be held to last three days, to which all the beautiful young maidens in the country were to come. When the sisters learned that they would go they began ordering their step-sister about... "We will soon be dancing with the King!" Cinderella did as she was told, but longed to go herself...*

Here, indeed, is the answer to all the women's prayers: A young man with eyes for the beauties in his realm, with a heart ready to be won, with a throne to give his bride. The sisters primp and preen and prepare to meet their Prince; Cinderella weeps, and begs her Stepmother for leave to go along. The woman is aghast:

> *"You go to the Feast? How can it be? You have no clothes and shoes, but you would dance? Nonsense!"*

Three times Cinderella cries and pleads, and twice Stepmother sends her off to pick the lentils from the ashes in the hearth. Like Psyche, enjoined by Aphrodite to separate a pile of grain, Cinderella too—with the help of all the creatures of the air— must sort things out before she can hope to meet her Eros in the Prince. This sifting through the ashes of one's life, "The good for the pot, the bad for the crop," is the torturous inner task that must precede true marriages of heart and mind. Note that nothing here is thrown away; the "bad" is recognized, and taken in. This is the work on Shadow, a task so painful only a Stepmother would demand that it be done.

> Paul spent his hour in recital of his lover's faults. They'd had one of their frequent fights and he wanted sympathy from me, support for his anger and his sense of being wronged. Instead, I asked him to examine his part in what transpired. How had he provoked her wrath, what might he have done to bring things to a different end? Such reflections were the last things on his mind and he snarled his disgust with me. What good was I if I couldn't take his side?

Cinderella never questions the rightness of her task. Always the good and pious child, she does as she is told, only to be turned away again:

> *Cinderella thought: "Now I can go to the feast!" But her stepmother said again: "No Cinderella, you may not go. You have no gown and you cannot dance. The King would only laugh!"*

Stepmother, in all her harshness, tells Cinderella one more necessary truth: the sackcloth and ashes of her grief are hardly proper dress for a royal ball, nor has she learned to dance while weeping on her mother's grave. If she's to meet The Prince she must put her mournful piety away.

> In the years in which I led discussion groups for single and divorced adults, I watched participants arrive in every stage of need, some still in mourning for the lover (husband, wife) they'd lost, or indeed had never had. Others were more ready to explore their newly "liberated" lives. The former frequently found sympathy and kindly nods of understanding in the group. Just as frequently they left the social hour alone. Something in their bearing said, "Not Yet," in words that all could understand.

Cinderella, having served her mourning time, is more ready than anyone can know. She calls upon her source of strength, and wastes no time in dressing for the ball:

When all had gone, Cinderella repaired to her mother's grave, where she wept and wished beneath the tree:

"Tremble, tremble little tree,
Gold and silver rain on me."

And the bird let fall a ballgown made of silver and of gold, and dancing shoes embroidered with the finest silk. Quickly Cinderella dressed, and just as quickly made her way to the palace of the King. There no one knew her in her golden gown...

We can imagine the fury and dismay of the sisters here, as they watch this lovely stranger dancing with the Prince. Why can't they catch his eye? They too have done just as mother said, but her motherly advice to them has been very different than she offered to the stepchild in their home. All of their energies and hopes have gone into selection of their clothes and jewels; into polishing their courtly manners and their nails. Their every hair is perfectly in place, but they've not been asked to do the inner work demanded of this "foreign princess" clothed in gold. How are they to understand the apparent ease with which she's captured the young man's heart? Neither Stepmother nor her daughters can recognize the hard-working maiden within the golden dress; they see only that she has what they have not.

> After years of agonizing work, Gloria is in reunion with her gifted inner Prince. She plays piano with a local band, sings through her days and steals the time to write the poetry she loves. Her husband, however, feels great envy when he sees her living out her gifts; he is tied to work that brings him little joy. While he rationally connects her blossoming with her therapeutic work he is nonetheless enraged; how dare she find the inner fire that still eludes his life?

Cinderella's sisters need not have envied her so much; for all her work, she is unprepared for the suddenness of her success, and flies away in fear:

*Cinderella danced until evening fell. But then she begged her
leave. The Prince wished to see her home but Cinderella fled
from him...*

How can Cinderella trust the love and admiration of the
Prince when her own father seems to see her not at all? Like his
wife and stepdaughters, he's failed to recognized the beautiful
young woman dancing at the ball.

> Bridget's father died when she was just thirteen, too soon to
> see his "little nurse" become the sprightly beauty she would
> grow to be. Today she is indeed a nurse, and she has mar-
> ried well, to a man who loves her more than she can quite
> believe. When they meet with friends she compares herself
> to all the other women in the room, and imagines that her
> husband finds her wanting in some way; they must be more
> desirable than she. She cannot find that father-voice within
> herself to say: You are the fairest in *this* land!

How is Cinderella's Prince to capture the mysterious, elusive
girl? He asks the man who ought to know her best:

*The Prince waited until Cinderella's father came, and told
him of the unknown princess hidden in the pigeon-house.
Her father thought: "Could it be Cinderella?" At that the old
man took an axe and chopped the pigeon-house to bits, but
no one was inside"*

"Can it be Cinderella?" We can hear the shock and wonder in
the old man's voice. As the veil of his denial slowly lifts, he must
contemplate his daughter in all of her nubility and charm. Can
this lovely woman be his little girl? When he attacks the pigeon-
house, and then the pear tree into which the Prince has seen the
maiden flee, it's as if the very nature of her feminine allure must
be destroyed before she leaves him for a younger man! When
we ask, "Who gives this bride to wed?" we are asking father no
small thing. His sense of loss at such a time may well evoke an
angry, vengeful "Stepfather," not unlike the "Stepmother" who is
forced to see her sons off into the world.

The father Kate recalls could not bear to see her sexuality emerge. When she eloped with the man who'd caught her eye, father's pain and grief made for an encounter he'd regret throughout his life.

> When Kate eloped, her father, furious, summoned her, her husband and his parents to a meeting at his home. He told her husband that he'd made a terrible mistake: his bride was lazy, disobedient, dishonest and a tramp. "She will be a rope around your neck for life!" The bridegroom was not inclined to "give her back," but the father-daughter rift took many years to heal.

Three times Cinderella ventures out to dance, and three times runs away, to hide once more among the ashes by the hearth. This retreat until the time is right, until the world feels safe enough for love, is part of the connection to the earth Cinderella demonstrates throughout this tale. There is safety in her dirty rags, and she'll hide in them until her doubts and fears release her into life.

> Anne's first forays into sexuality were frightening and harsh; she needed time then to withdraw into herself, to feel into her fear and rage, to learn to be more conscious of the woman she'd become. Accordingly, she made herself as unattractive as her natural beauty would allow: cropped her hair, gained thirty pounds, dressed in shapeless, faded clothes. She remained thus, to her family's dismay, for several years. When a gentle Prince appeared, with the capacity to see the woman hidden in the rags, she allowed herself to venture forth, to see and to be seen. The Prince has come and gone, but Anne has thrown her rags away.

Cinderella's Prince has made his choice, and as the festival comes to an end he determines not to let his disappearing partner go again:

> *[The Prince]...had seen that the palace steps were smeared with tar and pitch, and when she fled one of her golden slip-*

pers remained, caught in the sticky tar. The Prince held the slipper in his hand, and felt he would surely find the maiden now.

When morning came, he took the golden slipper to Cinderella's house, and showed it to her father, saying: "I will only wed the maid who fits this shoe." Then the sisters had some hope, for they had dainty feet.

Now begins the darkest portion of this tale, for while Cinderella hides herself and waits, her sisters try to fit themselves into her tiny shoe. As they try the slipper on their soft, uncalloused feet we hear that most dangerous of sounds, the well-intentioned voice of an ambitious mother-who-knows-best:

The elder of the two took the shoe into another room to try it on, her mother at her side. Alas, the slipper would not fit. But her mother handed her a knife and said: "Cut off your toe; you'll have no need to walk when you are Queen." This the maiden did, and despite her pain, forced her foot into the tiny shoe. The King's son, seeing her thus shod, carried her away to be his bride.

With the advent of an eligible Prince, mothers may see a life of ease ahead for their daughters—better lives, indeed, than they have had! They beseech their daughters to conform, to fit themselves into some pre-formed, perfect mold. There is freedom in security, they say, and time enough ahead for all your little quirks and dreams, for all the imperfections that make you who you are. There will be a time to take a stand, to run that race or write that book, time enough for wholeness when you are safely married to The Prince.

Perhaps modern women should know better, should know that a woman must accept herself—stand on her own two feet— if she hopes to find a Prince. But for all of that, one can't quite shut out the loud, collective voice that joins the desperate-mother voice within. "Reshape your nose," one hears. "File down your teeth and suck the fat out of your thighs; don't you know the competition's terrible out there?" When one's sense of self depends upon a Prince out in the world, no sacrifice of flesh, no loss of spirit feels too great.

What is tragic for the sisters in this tale is that their sacrifices are in vain. The Prince carries each of the pain-wracked maidens off in turn, only to be cautioned by the pigeons perched in Cinderella's magic tree: his bloodied bride is false. Now the younger of the sisters has her turn:

> *Then the second sister took the shoe into another room, where her mother waited with a knife. Again, the shoe was just too small, and the mother said, "Cut a bit off your heel...*"[6]

and once more, the Prince is warned as he carries the false sister by the hazel tree. Both young women offer up their mutilated feet, but the Prince has no desire for a bloodied, martyred bride.

> Linda recalls her mother when her family was young: "She had a joyful, playful side to her that she completely put away whenever my father was at home. None of us ever saw him laugh, and she assumed, I think, that laughter was not permitted in our house. I know she loved to swim and run and play out in the woods—other people told me this— but she simply let this go in an effort to 'grow up.' Eventually my father found his pleasure far from home; he told my mother that she'd ceased to move him long ago."

We must admire the determination of the Prince. He returns each of the injured sisters to her home, and asks Cinderella's father, one more time, for assistance in finding his true bride. Father must finally release his only child, his last reminder of the

---

[6]"Cinderella" has its source in seventh-century China, and this version of the tale may be a commentary on the practice of binding female feet. In China, highborn female children had their feet bound into tiny, lotus shapes. "The four smaller toes were folded under the sole, the whole foot was folded so the underside of the heel and toes were brought together." Women with bound feet were the essence of beauty and nobility. "Chinese men were conditioned to intense fetishistic passion for deformed female feet. Chinese poets sang ecstatic praises of the lotus feet that aroused their desire to fever pitch. The crippled woman was considered immeasurably charming by reason of her vulnerability, her suffering and her helplessness—she couldn't even escape an attacker by running away. (Walker 319).

wife and happy home he'd once enjoyed. His answer is so cruel and final in its disavowal that it serves to free Cinderella from his grasp. If she'd ever hoped to catch her father's eye, to win his love, that hope is surely gone with his reply:

> *"These maids have proved themselves untrue. Have you none other here beneath your roof?" "No," said the man; "only a scrawny servant-girl, here before my late wife died. She could not be your bride, I know." But when the Prince persisted, they called Cinderella in.*

For Cinderella and her Prince, what follows is the moment of surrender, recognition and a sense that all is as it's meant to be. Cinderella, her face washed clean of ashes and of grief, tries on the golden shoe that fits her perfectly:

> *When Cinderella stood to face her dancing partner once again, the King's son knew her then, and cried out in great joy, "That is my true bride!"*

Such moments are the stuff of which romantic literature and art are made.[7] Our beloved—the one we've dreamed of all our lives and have always known within ourselves—suddenly appears, fantasy made flesh. All of our ambivalence is gone, there is nothing left to do but bow to love, and pray that it will last.

As the Prince carries Cinderella off, we're told that Stepmother and her daughters become "pale with rage"—and pale, perhaps, with the sisters' loss of blood. One would think the tale could end right there: justice has been done, Cinderella has her man, her vain and selfish sisters have their mutilated feet and empty beds. But the worst is yet to come for the unhappy sisters in this tale:

> *On the wedding day, the false sisters came to join the royal train, hoping to find favor in their sister's eyes. On the way to the church they walked at Cinderella's side, the elder on the left, the younger on the right. The birds pecked out one*

---

[7]Cf. Haule, John, *Divine Madness: Archetypes of Romantic Love,* Boston, Shambhala Press, 1990.

eye of each. On their return from church, each walked on
Cinderella's other side, and the doves pecked out their
remaining eyes. Thus the sisters were struck blind, and were
punished for their falseness all their days.

Blindness has been a theme throughout this tale: Father, blind
with hope, seeks a second wife, then shuts his eyes to the
redoubled family grief within his home, to his daughters' needs
and the abuse being perpetrated out of unmet needs. His blindness in the dark further darkens every facet of his family's life.
The stepsisters, blinded by their envy of Cinderella's glowing
inner light, attempt to douse it with their cruel and mocking
taunts. And Stepmother, who can see very well what *Cinderella*
needs to bring her into life, cannot provide her daughters with
the guidance they require. She is too close to them to see them
as they are, too attached to their "well being" to offer them an
honestly reflective eye. As a "good" mother she has indeed been
blind, closed against the wisdom that the harsh, truth-telling
Stepmother can, and does, provide.

The pigeons in this tale, embodiments of mother-nurturance
throughout, provide the sisters with the sort of cursed gift a
Stepmother might give. What might blindness to the outer world
mean to the "vile, black-hearted" daughters we have come to
know? Their focus has always been "out there," on all the pretty
things that shine and glow in the material world, on all the treasures others might possess. They've had no insight, for to peer
inside themselves would have revealed an emptiness too terrible
to bear. Their sunlight gone, perhaps their helpless groping in
the dark will provide the inward shift of vision that their souls
require, the clear reflective eye always absent from their lives.

Cinderella's tale begins with her loving mother's death; her
time in rags and ashes prepares her for her life ahead. Her sisters face another sort of death. They can never be the prancing,
carefree careless girls they were; their hopes of dancing at
another ball are gone. What their lives will be we cannot know,
but the necessary darkness that precedes all inner work has
come. It is in this darkness that the sisters' tale begins.

CONCLUSION

THE LIFE AND DEATH OF STEPMOTHERS

I once worked with a young boy whose inner life was eloquently, silently, expressed in his mixing of colors. He'd turn the bare clinic treatment room into an alchemist's laboratory, the table spread with precisely ordered rows of small paper cups, each containing a rich dilution from his water color box. A pumpkin shaped bowl, the pot in which he "cooked" his magic brew, sat in the middle of his "lab." For months he'd mixed varied shades of blue, later oranges and reds, but always with an added touch of blue before the tincture was complete. Then one day something changed. Using every color on the table, he put all his energy and concentration into an effort to make black. The look of triumph on his face when he'd mixed true black—the vessel spilled a moment later, and the room was covered with his inky goop—was worth all the mess and scolding from the cleaning crew. The child's black held every color in his soul, every subtle shade of feeling that he'd touched on in his work.

Here, that child's work has been reversed. We began with the undifferentiated blackness of the abusive parent, but as we've come to know the Stepmother her colors have begun to tease apart. We've noticed her depressive blues, her rageful reds, her envious, sulphuric greens. The Stepmother constellated by the departure of a well-loved son is of a different nature than the

Queen confronted by her daughter's nubile innocence, and she is different still from the depleted wife who sends her children out into the world to starve. The devouring Witch, sweet as she might seem, is quite unlike the lonely widow who'll do anything to find her child a mate. There are so many colors in the black that to call the Dark Mother merely Bad is to do her grave injustice, and to see her not at all.

To know the Stepmother in her particularity is to understand her in the context of relationship and the stages of her family's life. While she is, archetypally, always present in potentia, she is colored by varieties of loss, by bereavement and by the special neediness of those around her. In the dark room, every color has its complement, its negative. To see Stepmother in her many hues is to understand her children, too, and to have a sense of mother-child mutual creation as their colors change along the way.

The Stepmother, as we've come to know her in these tales, is emblematic of whole family systems gone awry in the face of inevitable growth and change. Young men and women will come into bloom, will go off to see the world, will be carried off by young attractive mates. The aging, grieving parents that they leave behind may indeed act in harsh, unconscionable ways until the family's wounds begin to heal. At the very least, these once Good Parents will feel Stepmother moving into place, ready to wreak havoc in the home. Only consciousness and great restraint will keep her in her place.

Fathers, as we have seen, are far from separate from the darkness that befalls Stepmother's home. Father's weakness, in times of poverty and grief, is the shadow of his patriarchal strength; he mirrors the unconscious power of the Stepmother by becoming powerless in equally unconscious ways. Siblings, too, respond to family change in archetypal ways. In the face of cruel depletion they may embrace and guide one another through the woods; survivors of childhood abuse often recall a brother or a sister as their only friend, or think of their adolescent street gang as a band of "seven dwarfs," without whom they could not survive. Sadly, Cinderella's story also finds a place in many hearts. In a family economy of scarcity and loss, brothers and sisters can cause each other endless grief. The cruelty of children should come as no surprise; they are close to unmediated archetypal power, and to say that they are inherently aggressive, envious and cruel is no less strange or true than to think of them as innocent, divine and pure.[1] Like their parents, they carry all shades of Good and Evil in potentia in themselves. The sorts of family stress we've looked at here will touch on all the contradictions in a child's soul, some of which inevitably will be acted out.

In my work with abused children—of all ages—I have seen stages in the work not unlike the stages of bereavement that we've looked at here. One comes to know the Stepmother (and her family) slowly, and with considerable pain. Initially, the patient may feel numb, or beset by undifferentiated, global rage. There is a sense that something has gone wrong, but it is impossible to say just what it is. This black opacity seems to speak to primitive, pre-imagistic loss, a need so deep we have no words for it. One senses Stepmother somewhere in the room, but it's impossible to find her in the dark.

This initial sense of mystery is followed, sometimes very quickly, by a search for blame, a search entered into with great enthusiasm by patient and therapist alike. As is the case in the burgeoning Adult Child (of Alcoholics, Abuse, Incest) movement, one must declare oneself a victim, a Stepchild of one sort or another, before healing can proceed. One finds and names one's Stepmother, and in the naming finds a glimmer of one's own identity. There are therapies, it would seem, that never proceed beyond this point, as if to call oneself a Cinderella, a Hansel or a Gretel, were sufficient in itself. But the Stepmother, here, is only seen in silhouette, a dark collective shape against the red screen of the Child's rage. She has no color of her own.

Fairy tales provide a model for the third stage, the confusion and despair through which one must move before coming to the other side. Princess Margaret becomes a Dragon roaring on the

---

[1] Cf. Margaret Atwood's *Cat's Eye* (New York, Bantam, 1989) for an evocative portrayal of the cruelty to be suffered from one's childhood friends. A child needs to deal with much more than family in the course of growing up.

Heugh; Hansel and Gretel, and Snow White, must wander hungry through the woods. To save themselves, they must come to know the enemy (within/without), must meet her face to face. In this third stage one begins to differentiate among the many sorts of Stepmother. As she steps into the light her many colors can been seen, and she provides a mirror through which one can view oneself. She appears in fantasies and dreams, and in all the ways in which she's active in one's life. She speaks clearly now, sometimes, disturbingly, in one's own voice. She's acknowledged as an inner figure separate from (but in some way, related to) the mother one has always known.

As one works with her, the Stepmother becomes an image with a history, a past, a present and a future. She is no longer *The Stepmother,* a global, formless shadow, but one's particular Stepmother, shaped and colored by personal experience. She may change form and color as we look; she may lose some of her dark, unconscious power and begin to fade in her threatening intensity, but she'll remain an aspect of one's life. She only "dies," as she does in fairy tales, in that as we take her in as ours, and own some of her darkness, we become less hers.

Margaret is freed from her enchantment at the moment she acknowledges her loathsomeness; Snow White kills the Queen in an act of dark, Queen-like revenge, and quick-thinking Gretel does to the Witch just what the Witch would have done to her. When we draw close enough to Stepmother to really see her, perhaps, even, to learn from her, we are proof against her poison. Like Cinderella, we must sort through the ashes and the peas, separating good and bad before deciding to keep both. We recognize Stepmother in ourselves, and embrace her shadow. Thus, we rob her of her lethal power.

In bereavement, the fourth, and healing stage often involves the return of the loved one as a positive spiritual presence. The tortured, taunting ghost becomes a guiding light. So it seems to be with the image of the Stepmother. To know her is, if not to love her, then to value her for what she brings, and for what she's given to one's life. Like Hansel and Gretel, we turn back to the Witch's house to find a treasure there. The harsh one who sends Cinderella back to work may be giving her her greatest gift. Similarly, we all might thank the cold, rejecting Woodsman's Wife for our first hard push into the world, without which we might have missed some golden times. We might have missed the sticky-sweet devouring one who provided milk and cookies, at a price, when nothing else would do. Sometimes the price seemed almost fair. When we are feeling very young and pure Snow White's Queen protects us from our innocence, puts the poisoned apple of her knowledge in our hands when it's the last thing that we want, and exactly what we need. Bamborough's Stepmother toad remains to wake us from our inner lethargy, to remind us that our journey, at any given time, is more than likely incomplete.

A great deal is at stake here. If we can begin to see, and to see through, the Stepmother to the treasures in her house, we will have freed ourselves from our identities as helpless victims of her cruelty. We become her heirs as well, Childe Wynds and Gretels, Snow Whites and Margarets and Cinderellas all. There may be much of value in what she leaves behind.

But what becomes of those of us, mothers and therapists, who have felt the Stepmother working in our souls? Does some part of us die, do we forever feel the need to croak every time we see ourselves? Do we mourn the Stepmother when she goes? Like Cinderella's Sisters, perhaps some parts of Stepmother remain to rue the havoc that she's wrought, to look inside and heal the crippled blindness of her ways. But in another sense, the Stepmother dies whenever the bereavement that calls her into play has ceased to be. She's transformed when Childe Wynd returns, written off when Hansel and Gretel learn to feed themselves, dies outright when Snow White becomes a Queen. In killing off the Witch, in becoming who they truly are, her children bring a necessary healing to the home.

For mothers, the fantasy of being The Good Mother dies in the moment that Stepmother comes to consciousness. With the Dark Mother's death what can possibly be left? I would say, first, that the Stepmother's death, happy fantasy that it may be, is not likely to be permanent. She may return in different clothes, in another shape and color, but she will return, each time the needy child or some sense of loss calls her into play. In those moments, however, when The Stepmother seems gone for good, what may be left behind is neither Good Mother, nor Bad, but no Mother at all. A woman freed from the pull of both poles of the archetype can simply be a person, a woman who is sometimes called upon to mother, sometimes not. She is a woman who'll grow old, who will watch her children leave and, at times, need to be on hand for their return. When the Mothers die she will remain, watching the colors change and waiting for the story to unfold.

APPENDICES

THE TALES

The Laidly Worm of Spindleston Heugh

In Bamborough Castle, once lived a king who had a fair wife and two children, a son named Childe Wynd and a daughter named Margaret. Childe Wynd went forth to seek his fortune. Soon after he had gone the queen, his mother, died. The king mourned her long and faithfully, but one day while he was hunting he came across a lady of great beauty, and fell so much in love with her that he determined to marry her. So, he sent word home that he was going to bring a new queen to Bamborough Castle.

Princess Margaret was not very glad to hear of her mother's place being taken. However, she did not repine, but did her father's bidding. At the appointed day, she came down to the castle gate with the keys all ready to hand over to her stepmother. Soon the procession drew near, and the new queen came towards Princess Margaret, who bowed low and handed her the keys of the castle. She stood there with blushing cheeks, eyes cast to the ground, and said, "O welcome, father dear, to your halls and bowers, and welcome to you, my new mother, for all that's here is yours," and again she offered the keys. One of the king's knights, who had escorted the new queen, cried out in admiration, "Surely this Northern princess is the loveliest of her kind." At that the new queen flushed up and cried out, "At least your courtesy might have excepted me," and then she muttered below her breath, "I'll soon put an end to her beauty."

That same night the queen, who was a noted witch, stole down to a lonely dungeon wherein she did her magic, and with spells three times three, and with passes nine times nine she cast Princess Margaret under her spell. And this was her spell:

> I weird ye to be a Laidly Worm,
> And borrowed shall ye never be,
> Until Childe Wynd, the king's own son,
> Comes to the Heugh and thrice kiss thee;
> Until the world comes to an end,
> Borrowed shall ye never be.

So Lady Margaret went to bed a beauteous maiden, and rose up a Laidly Worm. And when her maidens came in to dress her in the morning they found coiled up on the bed a dreadful dragon, which uncoiled itself and came towards them. But they ran away shrieking, and the Laidly Worm crawled and crept, and crept and crawled till it reached the Heugh or rock of the Spindleston round where it coiled itself, and lay there basking with its terrible snout in the air.

Soon the country round had reason to know of the Laidly Worm of Spindleston Heugh. For hunger drove the monster out from its cave to devour everything it could come across. So at last the country folk went to a mighty warlock and asked him what they should do. The warlock consulted his works with his familiar, and told them, "The Laidly Worm is really the Princess Margaret and it is hunger that drives her forth to do such deeds. Put aside for her seven kine, and each day as the sun goes down, carry every drop of milk they yield to the stone trough at the foot of the Heugh, and the Laidly Worm will trouble the country no longer. But, if ye would that she be borrowed to her natural shape, and that she who bespelled her be rightly punished, send over the seas for her brother, Childe Wynd."

All was done as the warlock advised, the Laidly Worm lived on the milk of seven kine, and the country was troubled no longer. But when Childe Wynd heard the news, he swore a mighty oath to rescue his sister and revenge her on her cruel stepmother. And three and thirty of his men took the oath with him. Then they set to work and built a long ship, and its keel they made of the rowan tree. And when all was ready, they set out with their oars and pulled sheer for Bamborough Keep.

But as they got near the keep, the stepmother felt by her magic power that something was being wrought against her, so she summoned her familiar imps and said, "Childe Wynd is coming over the seas, he must never land. Raise storms, or bore the hull, but nohow must he touch the shore." Then the imps went forth to meet Childe Wynd's ship. But when they got near, they found they had no power over the ship, for its keel was made of the rowan tree. So, back they came to the witch-queen who knew not what to do. She ordered her men at arms to resist Childe Wynd if he should land near them, and by her spells she caused the Laidly Worm to wait by the entrance of the harbor.

As the ship came near, the worm unfolded its coils, and, dipping into the sea, caught hold of the ship of Childe Wynd, and banged it off the shore. Three times Childe Wynd urged his men on to row bravely and strong, but each time the Laidly Worm kept it off the shore. Then Childe Wynd ordered the ship to be put about, and the witch-queen thought he had given up the attempt. But, instead of that, he only rounded the next point and landed safe and sound in Buddle Creek. Then, with sword drawn and bow bent, he rushed up followed by his men, to fight the terrible worm that had kept him from landing.

But the moment Childe Wynd had landed, the witch-queen's power over the Laidly Worm had gone, and she went back to her bower all alone, not an imp nor a man at arms to help her, for she knew her hour was come. So, when Childe Wynd came rushing up to the Laidly Worm it made no attempt to stop him or hurt him. But just as he was going to raise his sword to slay it, the voice of his own sister Margaret came from its jaws, saying:

> O, quit your sword, unbend your bow,
> And give me kisses three;
> For though I am a poisonous worm
> No harm I'll do to thee.

Childe Wynd stayed his hand, but he did not know what to think, if some witchery were not in it. Then said the Laidly Worm again:

O, quit your sword, unbend your bow,
And give me kisses three;
If I'm not won ere set of sun,
Won never shall I be.

Then Childe Wynd went up to the Laidly Worm and kissed it once; but no change came over it. Then Childe Wynd kissed it once more; but yet no change came over it. For a third time he kissed the loathsome thing, and with a hiss and a roar the Laidly Worm reared back and before Childe Wynd stood his sister Margaret. He wrapped his cloak about her, and then went up to the castle with her. When he reached the keep, he went off to the witch-queen's bower, and when he saw her he touched her with a twig of the rowan tree. No sooner had he touched her than she shrivelled up and shrivelled up, till she became a huge, ugly toad, with bold staring eyes and a horrible hiss. She croaked and she hissed, and then hopped away down the castle steps. Childe Wynd took his father's place as king, and they all lived happily afterwards.

But to this day a loathsome toad is seen at times, haunting the neighborhood of Bamborough Keep, and the wicked witch-queen is that Laidly Toad.

Snow White

Once upon a time in the midst of winter, when the snow was falling softly from the sky, a queen sat by her ebony-framed window, sewing. When the Queen looked at the snow she pricked her finger with the needle in her hand. Three drops of blood fell upon the snow, and she thought, "I wish I had a child white as snow, as black as ebony, as red as blood upon the snow."

When a short time had passed she indeed had a daughter whose skin was white as snow, whose cheeks were red as blood, whose hair was ebony black. She called the little girl Snow White, and when the child was born, the Queen died.

A year later the King found himself another wife. She was beautiful, but very proud, and most jealous of the beauty that was hers. She had a magic looking glass, and she'd often stand in front of it and say:

> Mirror, mirror on the wall,
> Who is fairest of them all?"

And the mirror answered well:

> "You, my Queen, are the fairest of all."

Then the Queen would be satisfied, for she knew the mirror always spoke the truth.

But Snow White was growing more beautiful each year, and when she was seven years old was more lovely than the Queen herself. When the Queen asked her mirror:

> Mirror, mirror on the wall,
> Who is fairest of them all?

the mirror answered, in all truth:

> You, my Queen, are wondrous fair,
> But Snow White is fairer still.

The Queen turned green with envy and rage, and could not bear to have the child in her sight. Her hatred grew and grew, until she could no longer contain it in her breast. She summoned her huntsman, and bade him take Snow White into the woods and kill her there. "Bring me back her lungs and liver so that I might know that she is dead."

The huntsman took the child away, but when she began to weep he found he could not kill her after all. "Run away, dear child," he said. Then he stabbed a wild young boar that crossed his path, and took its lungs and liver to the Queen. Her cook salted them and served them to the queen, and the evil woman thought she ate the lungs and liver of Snow White.

But poor Snow White was alone in the deep woods, terrified by every rock and falling branch. She ran and ran, past wild beasts and over stones and thorns, but no harm befell her as she made her way. When it was almost dark she fell upon a cottage in the woods, and went inside to rest herself against the night.

The cottage was quite small, but neat and clean beyond belief. A table was set nicely with seven little plates, seven tiny spoons and forks and knives and seven little mugs. Against another wall seven beds were made up with coverlets as white as snow. Snow White was so hungry that she ate and drank a bit from every place; she did not wish to take too much from any one. She was so tired she tried every little bed, but none suited her until the last. She said her prayers, then fell asleep in the seventh little bed.

The owners of the cottage, seven dwarfs who mined the mountains for their ore, returned sometime after dark. By candlelight they could see that someone had been there to upset the perfect order of their home. Each exclaimed in turn, "Who has been sitting in my chair, eating from my plate, drinking of my wine? Who has been sleeping in my bed?" Then they saw the sleeping child, and were so taken with her beauty that none disturbed her rest.

The seventh dwarf took turns sleeping with his fellows through the night.

In the morning Snow White woke to face the seven dwarfs, and seeing they were friendly, told them of the wicked Queen and of the gentle huntsman and of how she came upon their cottage in the wood. The dwarfs said, "If you will cook for us and clean our house, if you will wash and sew and knit and make the beds, then you may stay with us. You shall have all you need as long as you are here."

Snow White agreed to all they asked, and stayed and cleaned and cooked their meals. But while they worked the mountains for their copper and their gold, Snow White was alone. The dwarfs, guessing how lonely she might be, warned her against letting anyone come in, "Your step-mother will soon learn that you are here. Beware!"

Indeed, the Queen, believing she had eaten the lungs and liver of Snow White, felt she was once again the most lovely in the land. She turned to her mirror and asked:

> Mirror, mirror on the wall,
> Who is fairest of them all?

And the mirror answered:

> You, my queen, are the fairest here.
> But beyond seven hills,
> Where the seven dwarfs dwell,
> Snow White is by far fairer still.

Then she knew that the huntsman had lied. Snow White was still alive! Her envy ate and ate at her, and she thought and thought again; how might she kill the child? At last, she disguised herself in ragged clothes and pretended to be an old woman, peddling her wares. No one could have known that it was she. She traveled over seven hills to the cottage in the wood, tapped on the window and called, "Pretties for sale! Pretties for sale here!"

Snow White, glad for company at last, greeted her with joy, "Good day, good day! What is it that you sell?"

"Pretty things for you," said the Queen, "bodice laces made of colored silk." At that, Snow White lifted the latch and let the peddler woman in the little house.

"My child, what a wreck you are! Come here, let me lace you properly for once." Snow White, having no suspicion, stood still and let the woman tie the laces round and round. She tied so quickly and so tightly that the child lost her breath and fell down where she stood. The Queen, certain now that Snow White was truly dead, thought, "Now I am the fairest in the land," and ran away.

When evening fell the seven dwarfs returned to find Snow White lying as if dead. They were horrified, but when they lifted her and saw the bodice laces tied so tight, they quickly cut her free. She soon began to breathe once more. When she'd come to life a bit, and told them what had passed, they scolded her:

"That peddler woman was the evil Queen! Be certain to let no one in when you are here alone."

But the evil Queen had learned the truth from her looking glass once more. As before, the magic mirror on the wall declared:

> You, my queen, are the fairest here.
> But beyond seven hills,
> Where the seven dwarfs dwell,
> Snow White is by far fairer still.

When she heard that she was filled with fear, for she saw that the child was still alive. She knew she must summon all her witchcraft to find a way to kill Snow White, once and for all. At length, she fashioned for herself a poisonous comb, and again changed into the shape of an old hag. She made her way across the seven hills to the cottage of the seven dwarfs. Tapping on the window, she called out, "Good things for sale! Good and pretty things for you!" Snow White, remembering the warnings of the dwarfs, bade her go away. Still, when she saw the lovely comb she let herself be fooled, and let the woman through the door. When the bargain had been struck the old hag said, "Come, let me comb you properly for once." Snow White had no suspicion. As soon as the comb had touched her raven hair the poison took effect, and she fell senseless where she stood. "Now my beauty," said the Queen, "you are gone at last," and with that she ran away.

With luck, the dwarfs were soon at home, and seeing Snow White in her death-like state immediately found the poisoned comb. When they removed the comb she quickly came to life, and told them what had passed. Again, they cautioned her to let no one in, no matter what temptation came her way.

But the queen had consulted her looking glass once more, only to hear these words:

> You, my queen, are the fairest I see.
> But beyond seven hills,
> Where the seven dwarfs dwell,
> None is so fair as she."

With this, the Queen was overcome with rage. "Snow White must die," she screamed, "even if I die as well!" She closed herself into a dark and secret room, a lonely place where no one ever came, and fashioned there a beautiful, but lethal fruit. The apple, white and red, was so lovely that all would want a bite, but anyone who tasted it would surely die.

When the fruit was ready the Queen dressed herself in peasant clothes, and made her way across the seven hills to the little cottage in the wood. When Snow White heard her come, she opened the window to chase the woman off. "I am forbidden to let anyone come in."

"Well and good ," said the Queen, "I shall sell my apples soon enough. Here, let me leave you one."

"No," said Snow White, "I may not take anything." "Do you think I'd poison you?" said the Queen. "Here, I'll cut the fruit in half; I'll eat the white cheek, and you can have the red." The fruit was so designed that only the red-cheeked half could kill; but this Snow White could not know. Reassured, she reached out for the lovely fruit, but hardly had it in her mouth before she fell down where she stood. The Queen gave her her darkest look, and laughed out loud, "Well, my lovely white-as-snow, this time your little friends will not bring you back to life!" Laughing still, she ran for home.

And to be sure, she asked her magic mirror once again:

> Mirror, Mirror on the wall,
> Who is fairest of them all?

To which the glass replied:

> My Queen, you are the fairest in the land.

At that, her rageful heart had rest, if, indeed, envy ever lets one rest.

When day was done the dwarfs came home, only to find the child dead. They combed her hair, loosed her ties and washed her face with water and with wine. Still, they could not bring

Snow White to life. They sat with her and wept for three long days, but when the time came to place her in the ground found that they could not. She was so beautiful, her cheeks as red as though she were alive.

At length, they fashioned a transparent coffin made of glass, and placed the coffin on a mountain top for all to see. Gold letters on the coffin told the world that the daughter of a king lay at rest within. One of the dwarfs stayed with her at all times, and the birds came to weep as well; an owl, a raven and a dove. And there the coffin stayed for many years, while nothing seemed to change within. Snow White remained as white as snow, as red as blood and with ebony black hair.

One day a prince came to the wood, and chanced upon the coffin in its mountain place. He read the golden letters, and longed for the beauty of Snow White within the glass. He wept and pleaded, and offered the dwarfs everything he owned if they would let him take the coffin off with him. They refused his gold, but at last they all took pity on the Prince, and gave him the coffin as a gift. His servants lifted it upon their shoulders and carried it away.

At length, the servants stumbled on a fallen branch, and the coffin nearly fell. The movement jarred the piece of poisoned apple free from Snow White's throat, and she came to life once more. She sat up and opened up her eyes, lifted the coffin's lid and cried, "Where am I?" The prince embraced her with great joy, told his tale and took her home to be his bride. She gladly went with him, and they planned a royal wedding to which all about would come.

The Queen, too, was invited to the wedding feast. She dressed herself with care, and asked her looking glass when she was done:

> Mirror, Mirror on the wall,
> Who is fairest of them all?"

The glass replied:

> My Queen, you are the fairest here,
> But the new young Queen is by far more fair."

The Queen swore and cried and moaned in utter misery. What was she to do? Her despairing heart gave her no peace and she went, despite herself, to join the wedding feast. There she recognized Snow White, who was expecting her. Iron dancing shoes had been set upon the fire; they were brought to the wicked Queen with tongs. She was forced to dance in the red-hot shoes, and dance she did until she died.

Hansel and Gretel

Once, on the edge of a great forest, there lived a poor woodcutter, his two children and his wife. His son was called Hansel and his daughter, Gretel. They had little enough in the best of times, and when a great famine struck the land, they could find no means to buy their daily bread. When night fell it brought the woodsman little rest, only worry of the day to come. "What are we to do?" he groaned to his wife, "How might we feed our children when we have nothing for ourselves?"

"Husband, hear me well," she said. "Tomorrow, we will take the children to the deepest woods, give them each a piece of bread and light a fire. We will leave them there, go about our work and not return. They'll never find their way back home, and we shall be rid of them for good."

The father was struck with horror at the thought. "How can I do such a thing? Wild animals will kill them in their sleep!"

"You foolish man," she said, "prepare our coffins then, for soon we'll all have starved."

As the night passed she gave the man no peace, and at length he did agree, weeping for his children all the while.

Hunger had kept the children up as well, and they overheard their stepmother's plan. Gretel wept in fear, but Hansel comforted the girl and said, "God will protect us, sister dear, and I will find a way to help." With that, he crept outside and found white pebbles gleaming in the silver light of a full moon. He stuffed his pockets with the little stones, then went back into his room to sleep.

Before the sun was up the next day, the woman roused the children from their beds. "Up, you lazy things! We must go to the forest and gather in some wood." With that, she gave each of them a single piece of bread, and said, "There's your dinner now, and remember, that is all you'll get."

Gretel kept the bread, since Hansel had his pockets full. When they all began to walk, Hansel stopped from time to time and looked back at the house.

His father cautioned him not to fall behind. "What are you looking at, my son?"

"I'm watching my white kitten on the roof; she wants to say goodbye."

His step-mother said, "Foolish boy, that's not your kitten on the roof, it is the rising sun."

No one noticed Hansel throwing pebbles on the path.

When they'd reached the deepest woods, the father told the children to gather up some twigs, and he lit a fire to keep them warm. When the flames were high, their stepmother bade them rest themselves. "When we're done our work, we'll come back to fetch you home."

Brother and sister rested by the fire and ate a bit of bread. They heard the strokes of a woodaxe and thought their father near, for he'd fastened a branch to a withered tree, where the wind would blow it back and forth. Thus falsely comforted they fell asleep, and when they woke it was darkest night. Gretel began to cry, but Hansel said, "Wait until the moon is high, then we'll find our way." And soon he took his sister by the hand and followed the shining pebbles he'd strewn along the path.

They walked all night, and when daylight dawned they saw their father's home. Knocking at the door, they surprised their father's wife. "You wayward children, wherever have you been? We thought we'd not see you again!" But their father leapt with joy, it had hurt him so to leave them in the wood.

Shortly thereafter famine struck the country once again, and the children heard their parents talking in the night. "All is gone," the woman said, "half a loaf of bread and that's the end of us. This time the children have to go, or we'll surely starve!"

The woodsman hung his head and thought, "Better to share with them until we have no more." But she insisted, and let him have no peace. As he had yielded to her once, he had to let her have her way once more.

Hearing this, Hansel tried to slip outside once more, but he found the door was locked. Still, he told his sister, "Dry your tears, dear Gretel, try to sleep. The good God will not forsake us now."

When morning came the woman roused the children from their beds, and gave them even less bread than before. As they walked into the wood, Hansel crumbled his small piece of bread, and stopped from time to time to throw crumbs upon the path. His father asked, "Hansel, what are you looking at now?"

"I'm looking at my pigeons on the roof," he said, "they want to say goodbye."

The stepmother scolded him, "You foolish child, that's not your pigeons, it's the morning sun." But as they walked Hansel spread his crumbs along the way.

The woodsman's wife led them ever deeper in the wood, until they'd found a place they'd never been before. A great fire was laid, and the woman bade the children rest themselves again, promising to fetch them when her work was done. At noon, the children shared their remaining bread, then fell asleep. When they woke it was darkest night, and no one came for them. Once more, Hansel comforted Gretel, saying, "Wait until the moon is high, then we'll find our way back home." But when the moon came up they found no crumbs; they had been eaten by the many woodland birds. The children told each other that all would soon be well, but they wandered deeper still into the wood, until two days had passed. Hungry and exhausted, they sat down beneath a tree and fell asleep.

On the third day they began to walk again, feeling that they must surely die. But at mid-day they were stopped by the beautiful song of a snow-white bird sitting on a bough. When the song was done the bird flew on before them, and they followed it until it led them to a little house built of bread and cakes. Even the windows were sweet, made as they were of sugar syrup. The children quickly set upon the house, Hansel gnawing on the roof, Gretel eating bits of window frame. Then a small voice came from within:

> Do I hear a little mouse?
> Who is nibbling on my house?"

The children, without pausing in their feast, replied,

> 'Tis only the wind,
> The heavenly wind."

and Hansel, who liked the tasty roof, tore down great chunks to feed himself. As Gretel pushed out a candy window pane, the door opened, and there suddenly appeared a woman older than the hills. The children were so frightened they stood frozen on the spot, dropping what they had in hand. To their great relief, the old woman nodded sweetly, and beckoned with her cane. "Come in, dear little ones, everything I have is yours." In the house, she fed them cakes and fruit and milk, then led them to two feather beds, laid with clean white linen cloth. Hansel and Gretel rested well, and felt they were in heaven after all.

But the old one was far from kind. In truth, she was an evil, child-eating witch, and she'd made the candy house to draw the hungry children in. When a child came close enough she'd kill it, cook it, and set her table for a feast. Like all witches, she had poor sight but a beastly sense of smell; she knew when children wandered near. When Hansel and Gretel approached she laughed with glee, and thought, "These little ones shall not escape again!"

When morning found the children still in bed, the witch admired the tasty morsels they would make. Then she pulled poor Hansel from his sleep, dragged him to a stable near the house and locked him in a little cage. His screaming woke his sister but she could not help. Instead, she was set to work, cooking food so that her brother could grow fat. "When he is fat enough, he'll make a hearty meal," the witch said to herself, and Gretel wept in vain.

Now Hansel had the richest food, while Gretel had naught but crab-shells and hard work. Each day the witch would go to

Hansel's little cage, and ask to see his finger so that she might judge his weight. Hansel, however, held out a little bone, and the half blind witch wondered if the child would ever grow fat. With four weeks she could wait no more, and ordered Gretel to fetch water for the pot. "Fat or lean, I'll have him on the morrow." Gretel wept and prayed, prayed and wept until the wicked woman silenced her, "Stop that noise, your tears won't help a bit!"

When morning came, Gretel had to light the fire beneath the big old pot.

"But first we'll bake," said the old witch, "come, see if the oven's hot and ready for the dough."

Gretel suspected that the witch would eat her too, and pretended not to know what was afoot. "I don't know how to judge the oven's heat." she said, "Could you show me how it's done?"

"You stupid thing," cried the witch, "look, you put your head in just like this." With that, Gretel pushed the old one from behind, and bolted fast the iron oven door. The witch howled and screamed for mercy as she burnt to death, but Gretel ran to set her brother free.

The children laughed and cried and danced in their delight, then, as they had no more to fear, they went back into the witch's house. They found it piled high with treasure of all kinds, pearls and jewels and gold, and they filled their pockets with whatever they could hold. "Let us be off," said Hansel, "and leave the witch's wood."

After two hour's walk they came upon a mighty waterway, too deep and wide to cross on foot. "I see no bridge or ferry, " said Hansel, "how are we to cross?"

But Gretel saw a white duck swimming by, and called to it for help. The duck came by. Hansel sat himself upon its back and called his sister to sit down as well. But Gretel waited, saying,"Together we're too heavy for this little duck. You go, then send her back for me."

Thus they crossed, one after the other, and soon found a path that led them to their father's house.

They ran into their father's arms, and all three danced and wept with joy. The man had had no happy thoughts since the day he'd left them in the wood. What's more, his wife had died. Now the children spread their gold and jewels about the house. Their worries came no more and all lived on in perfect peace and harmony. Thus ends my tale, and a mouse runs across the room. Catch it, and make yourself a fine fur cap.

Cinderella

The wife of a wealthy man fell ill, and was close to death. As her end drew near she called her beloved daughter to her side, and said, "My dear and only child, remember to be pious and be good. God, then, will protect you, and I shall watch from heaven and be ever near." With that, she died. The young girl visited her mother's grave each day and wept, remembering her mother's words. Winter came and went, and with the Spring the man had found another wife.

The woman had two daughters of her own, beautiful like she, but vile in temperament and black of heart. Bad times now fell upon the child of the poor dead wife, as the sisters plagued her with their insults and their ugly ways. They took her pretty clothes and bade her dress in rags and wooden shoes. "Where is the proud princess now?," they laughed, and had her work from dawn to dusk, cooking, washing, and lighting fires. They taunted her at every turn, and tossed her peas and lentils in the ashes so that she had to sit and pick them out once more. At day's end she could find no bed, but had to rest her weary bones by the kitchen hearth. As she was always covered by the fire's soot and ash, they called her Cinderella.

One day, when the father was about to travel to the nearest town, he asked his stepdaughters what he might bring them from the fair. "Pretty dresses," said the one, while her sister asked for emeralds and pearls. When he asked Cinderella, she replied, "Father, bring me the first branch to touch your hat as you ride home." And as it came to pass on the journey home, a hazel twig brushed against his hat , and knocked it off. This he brought for Cinderella, while he gave the sisters clothes and jewels. Cinderella thanked him, and planted the twig on her mother's grave. The hazel branch, watered by Cinderella's many tears, grew to a handsome tree, and a small white bird, nestled in the tree, granted Cinderella's every wish.

The King in those days had a son, and the son was looking for a bride. Accordingly, the King ordered that a feast be held, to last three days, to which all the beautiful young maidens in the country were to come. When the sisters learned that they would go they began ordering their stepsister about, "Cinderella, fix our hair and brush our clothes and fetch our finest jewels. We will soon be dancing with the King!" Cinderella did as she was told, but longed to go herself. She wept and pleaded with her Stepmother, but to no avail. "You go to the Feast? How can it be? You have no clothes and shoes, but you would dance? Nonsense!"

Cinderella, however, wept and begged again, until her Stepmother said, "Very well. Pick this dish of lentils from the ashes in two hours, and you may go with us." With that, Cinderella summoned all the pigeons and the doves and all the birds beneath the skies to help her with her task:

> The good is for the pot.
> The bad is for the crop."

Then all the winged creatures crowded round the hearth, and before an hour had passed all the grains had been sorted and gathered in a dish. The birds flew out again, and Cinderella thought, "Now I can go to the Feast!"

But her stepmother said again, "No, Cinderella, you may not go. You have no gown, and you cannot dance. The King would only laugh!" But Cinderella wept and wept, until stepmother said, "Very well. Pick two dishes from the ashes in one hour. Then you may go with us." And the stepmother thought, "Surely she cannot do that again."

But Cinderella once more summoned all the birds beneath the sky to help her with her task.

> The good is for the pot.
> The bad is for the crop."

And all the winged creatures crowded round the hearth to pick and pick, until two dishes of good grain were separated out. Cinderella thought, "Now I may certainly go to the feast!" But the stepmother said once again, "No, this will not help. You have no clothes and you cannot dance. You will only bring us shame." With this she turned away, for it was time to leave for the King's Feast.

When all had gone, Cinderella repaired to her mother's grave, where she wept and wished beneath the tree.

> Tremble, tremble little tree,
> Gold and Silver rain on me."

And the bird let fall a ballgown made of silver and of gold, and dancing shoes embroidered with the finest silk. Cinderella quickly dressed, and just as quickly made her way to the palace of the King. There no one knew her in her golden gown, and thought her a princess from a foreign land. Neither her step-mother nor her stepsisters thought of Cinderella; she could only be at home, sitting in the ashes by the hearth. Once the prince had seen Cinderella he would dance with no one else, nor let go her hand. "This is my partner," he would say to all who asked.

Cinderella danced until evening fell, but then she begged her leave. The prince wished to see her home, to see whence this lovely maiden came, but Cinderella fled from him and hid within the pigeon house. The prince waited until Cinderella's father came, and told him of the unknown princess hidden in the pigeon house. Her father thought, "Could it be Cinderella?" At that the old man took an axe and chopped the pigeon house to bits, but no one was inside. When all returned home they found Cinderella by the kitchen hearth, for she had fled the pigeon house, laid her gown upon her mother's grave, and run home to her ashes and her rags.

The next day, when the family had left for the second day of the feast, Cinderella went once more to the hazel tree, and wished:

> Tremble, tremble little tree,
> Gold and silver rain on me.

The gown was even more beautiful than that of the day before, and when Cinderella arrived at the feast all were amazed at her great beauty. The prince had waited eagerly for her to come, and when they began to dance he would not let go her hand. "This is my partner," he told all who would approach. When darkness fell Cinderella begged her leave, but the King's son followed her, hoping to learn whence she came. But when she'd reached her home she fled into the garden behind the house, and hid in a beautiful old pear tree there. The prince waited for her father to appear, and told him of his plight. The old man thought, "Could it possibly be Cinderella?" and he cut the tree down with his axe. No one was there, and when they reached the kitchen Cinderella lay asleep among the ashes once again.

When the third day came, parents and sisters went off early to feast, leaving Cinderella all alone. Once more, she approached the hazel tree, and called:

> Tremble, tremble little tree,
> Gold and Silver rain on me

And now she had a dress more beautiful than ever seen before, and slippers made of gold. The guests at the feast were speechless at the sight of her. The prince declared at once, "This is my partner," and would let no one else come near. When evening came, Cinderella fled once more, but this time the King's son was prepared to keep her close. He'd seen that the palace steps were smeared with tar and pitch, and when she fled one of her golden slippers remained, caught in the sticky tar. The prince held the slipper in his hand, and felt he would surely find the maiden now.

When morning came, he took the golden slipper to Cinderella's house, and showed it to her father, saying, "I will only wed the maid who fits this shoe." Then the sisters had some hope, for they had dainty feet. The elder of the two took the shoe into another room to try it on, her mother at her side.

Alas, the slipper would not fit. But her mother handed her a knife and said, "Cut off your toe; you'll have no need to walk when you are Queen." This the maiden did, and despite her pain, forced her foot into the tiny shoe. The King's son, seeing her thus shod, carried her away to be his bride.

But when they passed the tree growing on the grave, two pigeons nestled there called out to warn him of the blood within the shoe. Soon enough, when he'd seen the blood, he knew his bride was false. He returned her to her home, and resumed his search for the maid to whom the shoe belonged.

Then the second sister took the slipper to another room, where her mother waited with a knife. Again, the shoe was just too small, and the mother said, "Cut off your heel; you'll have no need to walk when you are Queen." The girl obeyed, and forced her bloody foot into the shoe. Holding back her tears of pain, she bowed before the prince.

Once more, the prince sat the maid upon his horse and carried her away to be his bride. But when they passed the grave, the pigeons warned him yet again. He saw blood dripping from the golden shoe, and knew his bride was false. This time, when he returned her to their father's home, he demanded of the man, "These maids have proved themselves untrue. Have you none other here beneath your roof?"

"No," said the man, "only a scrawny servant girl, here before my late wife died. She could not be your bride, I know." But when the prince persisted, above the protests of the father's wife, they called Cinderella in.

Cinderella washed her face and hands to come before the prince. Then she slipped the golden shoe upon her foot—it fit her perfectly—and stood to face her dancing partner once again. The King's son knew her then, and cried out in great joy, "This is my true bride!" They embraced, while her stepmother and stepsisters looked on, pale with grief and rage.

As the prince carried his true bride away, they passed the hazel tree once more. This time two white doves sang out good wishes for the happy pair, and came to sit on Cinderella's shoulders as she rode away. There they would remain until the wedding was complete.

And on the wedding day, the false stepsisters came to join the royal train, hoping to find favor in their sister's eyes. On the way to the church, they walked at Cinderella's side, the elder on the left, the younger on the right. The birds pecked out one eye of each. On their return from the church, each walked on Cinderella's other side, and the doves pecked out their remaining eyes. Thus, the sisters were struck blind, and punished for their falseness all their days.

BIBLIOGRAPHY

American Psychiatric Association, *Diagnostic and Statistical Manual of Mental Disorders (Third Edition)*.

Bettelheim, Bruno, *The Uses of Enchantment: The Meaning and Importance of Fairy Tales*. New York: Vintage Books, 1977.

Birkhauser-Oeri, Sibylle, *The Mother: Archetypal Image in Fairy Tales*. Toronto: Inner City Books, 1983.

Bowlby, John, *Attachment and Loss: Volume III, Loss*. New York: Basic Books, 1980

Cooper, J.C., *An Illustrated Encylopaedia of Traditional Symbols*. London: Thames and Hudson,Ltd., 1979.

Dieckmann, Hans, *Twice Told Tales: The Psychological Use of Fairy Tales*. Wilmette: Chiron Publications, 1986.

Elkisch, Paula, "The Psychological Significance of the Mirror." *Journal of American Psycholanalytic Assn,* 1957:5.243

French, Marilyn, *Her Mother's Daughter*. New York: Summit Books, 1987.

Graves, Robert, *The Golden Ass*. New York: Farrar, Straus & Giroux, 1951.

Haubrich, William S., *Medical Meanings: A Glossary of Word Origins*. New York: Harcourt Brace Javonovich, 1984.

Hillman, James, *Anima*. Dallas: Spring Publications, 1985.

____. *The Dream and the Underworld*. New York: Harper & Row, 1979.

____. *Puer Papers*. Dallas: Spring Publications, 1979.

_____. "Family: From Entrapment to Embrace." *The Texas Humanist,* March\April 1985.

Hunt, Margaret and Stern, James, Translators: *The Complete Grimm's Fairy Tales.* New York: Pantheon Books, 1944.

Hyde, Lewis, *The Gift,* New York: Vintage Books, 1979.

Jung, C.G., *Freud and Psychoanalysis. CW 4.*

_____. *Symbols of Transformation. CW 5.*

_____. *The Structure and Dynamics of the Psyche.* CW8.

_____. *The Archetypes of the Collective Unconscious.* CW 9i.

_____. *Mysterium Coniunctionis.* CW 14.

_____. *The Practice of Psychotherapy.* CW16.

_____. *The Development of Personality.* CW 17.

Klein, Melanie, *Envy and Gratitude, and Other Works.* London: Hogarth Press, 1975.

_____. *The Psychoanalysis of Children.* New York: Grove Press, 1960.

Kohut, Heinz, *The Analysis of the Self.* New York: International Universities Press, 1971.

Kubler-Ross, Elizabeth, *On Children and Death.* New York: MacMillan Publishing Co., 1983.

Masson, Jeffrey M. *The Assault on Truth:Freud's Suppression of the Seduction Theory,* New York: Penguin, 1984.

Melamed, Elissa, *Mirror,Mirror: The Terror of Not Being Young.* New York: Linden Press, 1983.

Miller, Alice *The Drama of the Gifted Child* New York: Basic Books, 1981.

Moffat, Mary Jane, ed. *In the Midst of Winter: Selections from the Literature of Mourning.* New York: Random House, 1982.

Neumann, Erich, *The Child.* Ralph Manheim, Translator; New York: Harper & Row, 1973.

_____. *The Great Mother,* Ralph Manheim, Translator; Princeton: Princeton University Press, 1963.

Roth, Philip, *Portnoy's Complaint,* New York: Bantam Books, 1969.

_____. *The Facts,* New York: Farrar, Straus & Giroux, 1988.

_____. *Patrimony,* New York: 1991.

Samuels, Andrew *The Father,* New York: University Press, 1985.

Schectman, J.M. "Hansel and Gretel Revisited: Little to Bite and to Break," *Psychological Perspectives* 1989, 21:30.

_____. "The Stepmother in Fairy Tales: Bereavement and the Feminine Shadow", in *Fathers and Mothers,* P. Berry, ed. Dallas: Spring, 1990.

Sidoli, Mara, "De-integration and Re-integration in the First Two Weeks of Life," *Journal of Analytical Psychology,* 1983, 28:201-212.

_____. *The Unfolding Self.* Boston: Sigo, 1989.

Stein, Murray, *In Midlife.* Dallas: Spring Publications, 1983.

Stein, Robert, *Incest and Human Love.* Dallas, Spring, 1973.

Tatar, Maria, *The Hard Facts of the Grimm's Fairy Tales.* Princeton: Princeton University Press, 1987.

Von Franz, M.L., *Puer Aeternus,* Boston: Sigo Press, 1981.

Walker, Barbara G., *The Woman's Encyclopedia of Myths and Secrets.* San Francisco: Harper & Row, 1983.

Weisner, David and Kahng,Kim, *The Loathsome Dragon.* New York: G.P.Putnam's Sons, 1987.

Wette, Adelheid, Librettist, "Hansel Und Gretel", an opera by Engelbert Humperdinck, 1891.